PAPUA PILOT

Flying the Bible to the Last Lost Peoples

By Paul Westlund
with Dane Skelton

xulon
PRESS

PAPUA PILOT
by Paul Westlund with Dane Skelton

Printed in the United States of America

ISBN 9781626973022

www.xulonpress.com

TABLE OF CONTENTS

FOREWORD

by Steve Saint

Mincaye and I were sitting on stools at the front of the auditorium in the first speaking occasion that I had been involved in since being badly injured in an accident in 2012. As we began our speaking engagement that night up in Gainesville, Florida, I asked Mincaye to tell the people in the audience how he became a follower of God's trail.

Mincaye had something on his mind that was quite different. He began to explain in great detail what his journey to Florida had been like. He had heard of my injuries and wanted to see me, so he started out, walking jungle trails to the airstrip, flying in the missionary plane to Shell Mera, catching a ride to the cold city of Quito, then flying to "the foreigner's place." He wanted to make sure that the audience would share in his significant travel adventure.

In the land beyond roads the world is very different from what most readers of this book can imagine. I remember once walking a jungle trail—I had gotten to the bottom of probably the 15th major ridge that we had climbed that day and I was just absolutely exhausted. I set up my little GPS and realized that we were less than one-half of the way to our destination. I really wasn't sure that I'd be able to make it. And then, as I was sitting beside the little Ecuadorian jungle stream, bathing my feet before putting them back in my rubber boots to continue our day-long trek (we were trying to get to Nemonpade, where I lived with my family), I heard an airplane off in the distance. It had probably come from Quiwado and was heading over to another jungle Waodani village called Tzapino.

As I listened to the little plane, I realized that in less than five minutes it would have traveled more than twice as far as I would cover in this entire excruciating painful day—and I was only half-way there!

I remembered again why the Waodani had asked me—demanded me—to come and live with them. They wanted me to teach them how to offer medical, dental, and optometry services to their people. (the medicine thing, the tooth thing, and the eye thing) But first they thought it was more important that I should teach them to fly. The Waodani said, "How can we teach (meaning the Gospel) our people if they don't see us well when we get there not understanding the airplane thing?" It has been an ongoing project and we are halfway there.

The stories in this book are about the "go" in our great commission. Jesus told us to go into all the world so that everyone would have a chance to hear the plan of salvation that God has made for all of us who will accept it. But the "go" is the part that most of us forget. If we don't go we can't share the message or teach them to share it with their own people so the next generation will stay involved.

You will enjoy Paul Westlund's stories—I'm sure they will captivate you as they have captivated me. Telling the stories is one of the primary ways we can interest people to share God's hope with the rest of the world.

DEDICATION

To Mr. & Mrs. Howard Westlund

To LaVonne, Joy, Mark, and Jadyn

PAPUA PILOT GUIDE

The CHAPTERS in this book are a series of snapshots of Paul Westlund's life as a Mission Aviator, taken from interviews we recorded as he paged through his log books. The POSITION REPORTS are from brief prayer requests he emailed a few times a month. They give the reader a feel for the day-to-day reality of a Mission Pilot. The CHECKLISTS at the end of each chapter are questions designed to help the reader learn from Paul's experiences and generate discussions with friends.

Finally, the book doesn't include much about the four most important people in his life: his wife LaVonne, his daughter Joy and her daughter Jadyn, and his son Mark. Paul would want you to know how much he treasured them and that their story deserves a book of its own.

It has been one of the greatest privileges of my life to collaborate with Pilot Paul of Papua on this project. He was a gifted aviator, a compelling story teller, and a dear friend. I hope that you will hear his voice and feel his passion as you read.

Dane Skelton

PART ONE

WHY WE FLY

With LaVonne, Mark and friends in a PC-6.

1

THE MISSIONARY'S MOTORCYCLE

I t all began in a motorcycle shop. My dad was a pastor, but out of necessity he was also a pretty good mechanic. I grew up helping him work on the family cars, and by the time I was seventeen I could sort out most mechanical problems that came my way. I tried for a while to be a pastor like my dad, but a frustrating year at a Christian College, where I spent more time fixing classmates' cars than studying (I'll never get Greek and Hebrew), landed me in a motorcycle shop west of Chicago. Though I had already committed myself to being a missionary, I wasn't pastor material, and I didn't quite know how that would work out.

One day a man named Doug Deming walked into the motorcycle shop looking for parts for an old Honda step-through motorbike. The parts were a bit hard to find. As I thumbed through the catalogues, I started asking him questions:

"So does your wife ride this? Your daughter?" In my world no *guy* would ride this wimpy little thing.

"No, I ride it."

"You ride it?" I stepped back a little bit as I asked, not wanting to get the same disease and start riding these little bikes. "So where do you ride it?"

"Peru"

"Peru, Indiana, or where?"

"Peru, South America. I'm a Mission Pilot. I ride the bike to the hangar every day and fly missionaries to wherever they need to go."

"Could you say that again? You fly missionaries around?"

"Yes, I work as a pilot down there with a mission, and I fly missionaries around."

"Whoa!" My eyes widened, my heart sped up, and sparks flew around in my head. So, while I looked up the parts I asked questions, and this guy told me stories about being a Missionary Pilot.

After Doug left I walked into the boss's office. "Look, I don't know, but I think this might be my two week notice. I'm going to try to get into this school called Moody and go become one of these Missionary Pilots."

Two weeks later I was gone. Now I'm the guy riding the step-through motorbike. And if I met an interested young person in a motorcycle shop today, these are the stories I would tell.

Checklist:

✓ What circumstances brought you to your current job?

✓ What would make you leave it?

Helio Courier on final approach.

2

WHY WE FLY

Papua, Indonesia

" Aiieeeeeeee! Aieeeeee! Ohhh aieeeee!" The shrieks jolted me so violently I almost yanked the yoke in the middle of the turn to base. The little Papuan woman beside me had been quietly polite most of the trip, but now her moaning, wailing screams filled the cockpit, filled my mind, filled the sky with anguished fear. I shot a glance out under the banked right wing and then the left, looking for other planes, a bird, anything that might have frightened her and threatened us at such a critical point in the approach to the tiny mountain airstrip. Nothing was there; nothing endangered us. Then I fixed my eyes back on the runway, dropped in the last notch of flaps, made the turn to final, and saw what had set her off. Her family, her friends, her whole village waited for her at the loading area. She had kept her grief in check as her husband's simple coffin had been loaded in the back. She had not spoken of him to me on the flight or looked over her shoulder to make sure he rode securely. Now she was undone. The sight of her family had collapsed the cover over a deep well of hopelessness, and the endless grief poured out.

We weren't on the ground yet. We weren't safe. I was in the most critical phase of landing and needed all of my concentration to put the plane down without crashing. Focus was hard to come by with that much grief energy pouring out beside me. So I did the only thing I could. I screamed out the landing checklist to God.

"Oh God, the mixture is rich! Oh God, the prop is set! Oh God, the trim is set! Oh God, the gear is down and locked! Oh God, the flaps are set! Oh

---

Position Report - Peanut Farmers & Pilots

Imagine you are a peanut farmer in a remote village far away from any towns. In fact, you have never even seen a town before because getting there would take four days walking over rough terrain.

Your neighbor is also a peanut farmer. In fact, so is everyone in your village. You can't very well sell your peanuts to your neighbor when he also grows peanuts. So, you and your village struggle to survive, with very little to eat and very few supplies. You are among the poorest of the poor in a remote village in Southeast Asia.

Now imagine a Mission Pilot flies to your village regularly and picks up your peanuts for you. He loads them on his plane and takes them to the market in town. Then he buys supplies for you with the money from the sales. He is able to get four to five times what you are able to sell it for in the village.

Your world is changed. Now you can buy things that weren't available to you before: rice, machetes, building supplies, noodles, and more ... Now, you are inspired to grow more peanuts because you are able to see fruit from your hard labor. You are still among the world's poor, but your lifestyle has seen a significant change.

Pilot Paul in Papua

God, we are committed to land!" It didn't matter that the landing gear is fixed on the Helio Courier I was flying or that I'd already worked through most of the checklist. I matched her scream for scream, volume for volume, until I felt the main wheels thump into the turf and lowered the tail because it helped me concentrate. Then I added power and the big Lycoming engine pulled us up to the loading area. She continued crying and wailing as I pulled the mixture to full lean and watched the prop stop. I took a deep breath, reached over and unbuckled her seat belt, and opened the door. She poured out into the arms of her waiting loved ones who picked up her lament and surrounded the plane with tears.

Death is always hard. But it is hardest for those who have no hope. I have seen Papuan people bite the fingers of dead family, trying desperately to wake them up. Death terrorizes them.

I know too that not long ago my friends in the Ketengban region and similar areas throughout Papua were so frightened of the spirit world that anything strange induced even stranger behavior. If a mother died in childbirth, her child might be killed and buried with her. If twins were born, one or both might be thrown in the river because something obviously went wrong; they felt that only evil spirits could have produced twins. Or if one twin died, the other might be killed and buried with him. When women went into labor they were taken to a birthing place down the mountain, downstream on the river, away from the village, and away from all men. All of the men in the village would then seclude themselves in houses for men only. When the baby crowned, a signal came and the men covered their faces and ears, closing up all entries to the body, lest the spirits set loose in this fearful event involving the blood of females should invade them as well causing physical weakness and loss of power, perhaps even death.

Then there is the tribal warfare, the brutality against women, and the cannibalism. These and many other odd, bizarre, or tragic things were common among some of the Papuan people groups until they began to hear and understand the message of Jesus in their own language.

It can take many years, many sacrifices on the part of the translators and their families, some of which you will hear about in this book. But when the grace and truth of God manifested in his Son Jesus Christ finally dawns on them, when they begin to understand that God loves them and that they no longer have to fear death, that faith and love can overcome spiritism and brutality. Joy is born.

Aviation plays an incredibly significant role in that joy. It transforms weeks of dangerous travel for missionaries and natives into minutes. It can open the world of education and opportunity and development to the forgotten peoples of the planet. It means that simple injuries and illnesses can be treated before they become life threatening infections in the Petri dish conditions of the equatorial jungle, and it makes the life-giving message of Jesus accessible. That is why we fly.

*****

Checklist:

✓ What is your life's purpose?

✓ Why did you choose it?

The Piper Tomahawk. Photo credit: Margo Harrison / Shutterstock.

3

TWIRLING TOMAHAWK

Pennsylvania

A tiny Amish farmer, his mule team hooked to a threshing machine, is spinning clockwise in my windshield. The scene is seared into my memory. Every time the farmer reaches the twelve-o-clock position, he's hundreds of feet closer, the golden color of his field filling the windscreen more with each rotation. The ailerons are neutral. The elevator is neutral. The power is pulled back, and I'm pushing for all I'm worth on the right rudder, doing everything by the book, but the airplane won't stop spinning. In less than a minute we are going to make a smoking hole in the ground.

In 1982, at age 28, I was taking any aviation job I could get in order to build time and experience. I preferred to work as a pilot/mechanic, but at the time I was working as a flight instructor, flying a two seat, training aircraft called the Piper PA-38 Tomahawk. The Tomahawk was introduced in 1978 to replace the Piper Cherokee. It turned out not to be such a great replacement, but just how dangerous it was wasn't clear to me until the day I turned it over to a new certified flight instructor (CFI). I'd found a better job and was checking out Royce Wingert, the new guy, in the plane.

The Tomahawk has very nasty, unpredictable stall spin characteristics. Instead of buffeting a little bit and nosing over like the Cherokee it was meant to replace, the Tomahawk would shudder, the wings would oil-can, changing shape under load, and the airplane would rapidly drop a wing into a spin. Research into the Tomahawk's problems had shown many quality control issues in an airplane that had been rushed to market. The worst revelation was that the aerodynamic problems were inconsistent. The

> **POSITION REPORT- Flying Crocodiles**
>
> Crocodiles are legal to trade out here. I picked some up in Dabra yesterday to earn a little revenue on the way back to Sentani. The more we can earn like this the less we have to charge our missionaries for flights. The farmers dehydrate them a little, truss them up, crate them, and load them on the plane for you. So I was just checking. We're talking five foot lizards with big teeth here folks, so I was checking, had my head inside the back left loading door of the Helio Courier, lots of people watching.
>
> A smaller box on top of the crates shook. Then it jerked and the top popped off. I had crocodiles on the brain. I jumped back fast and hit the back of my head on the top of the door frame, then fell to the ground and scooted back from the plane. Out popped a chicken that landed on the ground, trying to make an escape.
>
> The crocodile farmers got a good laugh out of that. Now they call me "the pilot who runs from chickens."
>
> Pray for the Chicken Pilot

same maneuvers produced different behaviors in different airplanes. Thus the PA-38 earned its nickname: The Traumahawk.

Well, we weren't going there. Spinning any airplane is a thing requiring expertise and preparation. Parachutes must be worn, exit strategies must be rehearsed, and the airplane must be approved for spins. Though the Tomahawk is certified for spins, Royce and I didn't plan to get anywhere near that part of the performance envelope. We were just going to do some low speed air work to familiarize him with the airplane, and then I would move on to my new job.

With Royce in the left seat, we took off and climbed to four thousand five hundred feet, leveled out, trimmed the airplane, and then slowly brought the power back and the nose up to enter the area of slow flight that every pilot has to be familiar with in order to land. Suddenly, without warning, the left wing stopped flying, the nose dropped, and the airplane entered a rapid counterclockwise spin.

A quick look at Royce and the controls told me he was doing everything by the book. The ailerons were neutral, the elevator was neutral, the throttle was back, and even though my right foot was nearly pressing a hole in the floor, I needn't have worried. He had the right rudder pedal fully deflected, exactly the control input called for to correct a left hand spin. Nonetheless that Amish farmer was getting bigger all the time.

"It's not coming out! You have the airplane!" Royce called into the intercom.

Now *I'm* doing everything right: ailerons, elevator neutral, throttle out, hard right rudder. Yet we were still spinning like a silver maple seed on its short trip to earth.

One of the things my mission organization emphasizes when training new bush pilots is to be ready for anything. Knowing that, and wanting to be the best pilot I could be, I had taken spin training a few years prior to that day in the twirling Tomahawk. So I wasn't panicked, but I knew it was time to try something that wasn't in the handbook, or get ready to meet my Maker.

I started moving things around. I deflected the ailerons right and left. Nothing! I shoved the yoke in and pulled it out. Nothing! I even stepped on the left rudder; the farmer only twirled faster with that one. One thing you don't want to do in a spin is add power. The airplane is already in a dive. It won't take much to rip the wings off. But power was all we had left.

Full power on the little four cylinder Lycoming, giving a blast of air over the full right rudder, and just as fast as we had entered the spin, we were out of it, zooming low enough to catch the farmer's attention who looked up briefly and then back to his team.

I glanced at the altimeter and took a deep breath, thirteen hundred feet. We had fallen over three thousand feet in a very few seconds.

I looked over at my new friend and implored, "Take me back to the airport, Royce. I am never going to fly one of these airplanes again!"

One of the worst mistakes I ever made as a young pilot was to shake that event off and walk away. Had I been thinking of my fellow aviators I would have realized, "Hey, we just survived a near-fatal loss of control by doing something that is not in anybody's manual. We need to report that."

*****

Checklist:

✓ One of the reasons pilots keep logbooks is to remember events like this one and learn from them. If you had a logbook for life, what is the first lesson you would write down?

✓ Proverbs says, "Get wisdom and with all your getting, get understanding." (Proverbs 4:7) Pilots get wisdom from other pilots. Where, other than the Bible, do you find wisdom?

With one of my Papuan friends in traditional dress.

4

LOSING MY PROFESSIONAL PILOT'S FACE

Papua, Indonesia

I couldn't believe it. *I get paid to do this?* I said that to myself so that the translator flying with me wouldn't hear. The big Lycoming six-cylinder was purring contentedly up ahead, all of my instruments were in the green, the early morning air was unusually smooth, and the view out of my "office window" was nothing short of spectacular. Brilliant sunlight splashed across the tips of granite green peaks that shot themselves up like a warrior's spears, piercing the thin blue armor of sky. Water falls leaped from the mountain's sides and dove for the deep green valleys below, hurling rainbows in their wake as they disappeared into impenetrable foliage. Soft white clouds, lying low in the valleys, slowly dissolved as the sun reached down beneath the peaks and pulled back the covers on a new day.

I get paid to do this? I said once more to myself and tried to hide the silly grin on my once professional pilot's face as I made the descent toward our destination and set up for a close inspection of the airfield.

That's when I saw it, crumpled white and light green, lying limp and dull against the forest floor. *What's that?* I thought. I turned and made another pass. *O Lord! That's an airplane! That's what's left of one of those aircraft called an Islander.* The smile ran away from my face then. *This is serious business. Bad things can happen out here, kid. You better get your game on; you better be paying attention.* I

Position Report - A Mission Pilot needs to:

Be like the fold-up multi tools they wear on their belt: flexible, versatile, and capable of changing a spark plug or fixing a botched landing.

Be ready for anything: the landscape that looks like we are flying through the beautiful pages of *National Geographic* is deceptively hostile. If the engine quits and you drop through the jungle canopy and survive and make it out, you will be able to write one of those miracle stories for *Reader's Digest*.

Be aware of his surroundings as he maneuvers the plane between mountain ridges, dodging clouds, keeping an eye out for flashes of lightning, and an ear out for radio calls about weather problems or of patients that need help.

Take a close, close look at that 360 yard dirt strip he is about to land on. Drop off the translation couple and pick up produce and two sick people to go to the hospital. On takeoff, don't let a windshield full of bats spooked out of the tree they were sleeping in spook you into the trees.

Pilot Paul in Papua

focused in hard on the task at hand: to get the airplane on the ground and parked as best and professionally as I possibly could.

The Apostle Paul once wrote to his protégé Timothy, "Keep your head in all situations ..." That is good advice for anyone, but especially for bush pilots. Our "situations" often run from the super serious to super comical in a single day, as my first flight with a translator revealed.

The journey from student pilot to Mission Aviator is a long and difficult one. Mine had taken ten years of hard work from the first flights with Moody Aviation School all the way through eighteen hundred hours of experience and training to the Airline Transport Pilot rating.

All of that work, all of that training and expense and struggle to make it out to the field was, and still is to me, for the compelling work of Bible Translation. When people are finally able to read and understand the message of Jesus in their own language, it gives them hope beyond their wildest imagination.

The main goal is to make sure that the translator can get to the location in one piece. If something bad happens to a translator, all of the work on a new translation can be lost. I had worked hard to be the best pilot that I could be so that would never happen. Now I was taking my first translator to his assignment in the field, and I was so happy I was almost giddy, until I saw that wadded up airplane.

Once we rolled to a stop and the prop stopped turning, I set the park brake, stepped out of the airplane, and lost my professional pilot face for the second time that day. I had never been in a Papuan mountain village before. It was *National Geographic* in living color right in front of me. The men were wearing their only clothing: tall, thin, conical shaped gourds, tied just below the waste and pointing straight up. The women were in tiny grass skirts. That was it. *Nothing else.*

It was more than this modest, Midwestern preacher's boy could take! I joke with my friends, that where I come from we don't even take *showers* without our underwear! I could feel my face going full red. I turned around and stuck my head in the cockpit and studied my aviator's chart to figure out where we were going next. I wrote in my log book. I inspected the airplane! Anything I could do to keep my eyes off of the people. I couldn't eat the rest of the day. I was just toast! *You are not in Kansas anymore, Toto,* I thought. *Have I landed on Mars or something?* It took a long time for me to regain my composure.

*****

Missionaries all over the world are as sensitive to criticism as anyone. We've taken stinging criticism from anthropologists and sociologists for importing Western values into cultures that don't need them. So when Bible Translators began working with Papuan people groups, they didn't talk about clothes. But the Papuan people are like anybody else on the planet. When they see an improvement on life, they want it. One day a translator friend of mine named Andrew who had been welcomed into the Ketenban community was walking along a trail with two Ketenban men. One of the men spoke.

"Andrew, you say that you love us, but we aren't so sure about that."

"Uh, OK. That makes me sad. Why do you say that?" he cautiously replied.

"You say that you have something good and you want to share it with us, but we think you are holding out on us."

"Oh. Well that may be true, but I'm sure it is not intentional. Can you explain what you're talking about?"

One of the men reached over and gently rubbed the cloth of Andrew's shirt between his fingers and said, "This looks like it might be warm. We get cold here at night, and we don't have anything like this."

"Well then, we'll have to see if I can help you buy some. Would you like that?"

The men smiled, "Now we know you love us."

Today, with better transportation and the availability of baled, used clothing for pennies on the pound, more Papuan people groups are wearing clothes. They really like wearing them because of the warmth and because it helps them feel like they are part of the rest of the world. But they weren't wearing them on that day and I was embarrassed.

Now, after twenty-five years on the field, the Papuan people are very dear to me. I no longer notice what is on their bodies, but what is in their hearts. And I keep my professional pilot face on ... most of the time.

*****

Checklist:

✓   What is the most sobering experience you've had lately?

✓   What is the benefit of "keeping your head in all situations"?

27

Every kilo counts on runways like this. Photo credit: Tim Harold.

5

PUSHING THE MARGINS AND LIVING TO TELL

Maluku Islands, Indonesia

The voice on the other end of the radio, a missionary from another organization that we work with a lot, was polite but urgent. "Paul, we are really in a bind. My wife Marie is sick. I'm pretty sure it's malaria again. And the boys have to get back to school in the States. Our mission's airplane is down for repairs. It will take us a week by boat to get out to your preferred pick-up point. By then the boys will have missed their flights home, and I don't know what kind of shape Marie will be in. Can't you make an exception?"

I felt for my friend. I knew what malaria could do. I knew how expensive and complicated it was to miss the first leg of an international flight with multiple connections. On the other hand, I considered Willem and Echo and Neil and Dave, all friends, fellow Mission Aviators, and all dead because, in trying to meet an urgent need, they pushed the margins too far.

The difference between stopping a five thousand pound aircraft landing at fifty nautical miles per hour (knots) and stopping one landing at fifty-two knots may not seem significant, but it is exponential. Each additional unit of speed multiplies the roll-out by hundreds of feet. Each kilo of weight requires just so much distance for a safe takeoff. The numbers are hard, cold, and inflexible. Ignore them, try to fudge them, and you and your passengers will pay, perhaps with your lives. I was flying the twin engine Piper Aztec at the time, a very capable airplane, but larger and heavier than the single engine airplanes that their airstrip was built for. Our safety margins required a minimum of six hundred meters for the Aztec. Their strip was only five hundred fifty meters long.

> **Position Report - A Mission Aviator must:**
>
> Smile, laugh, and realize the good fortune of doing the Great Commission and seeing people know "What a Friend We Have in Jesus" far outweighs the fatigue you are feeling as the tropical afternoon fades.
>
> Deal with pigs that run onto the airstrip chased by their owners.
>
> Sleep under a net to keep the malaria mosquitoes from using your face as a runway. And eat what you are given. Chicken feet? Yes, spit out the bones.
>
> Keep track of the translators' needs and also the myriad details of checking the plane and mail bag and medicines and know where to stop for fuel to get home.
>
> Pilot Paul in Papua

I didn't want to go.

"Hey look, I understand, and I want to help. But I can't make a call like this one on my own. Let me call our chief pilot down in Sentani and get his input. I'll call you back in a couple of hours and let you know what he says."

The situation had a precedent. About a year prior I'd received a similar request. I called Syd Johnsen, acting chief pilot while Tom Beekman was on furlough, and he said, "You make the call. If it's too marginal, say no." I said *No*. So calling the chief pilot was a slam dunk. The answer would definitely be *No*.

I put in the call, expecting it to take about three minutes. Forty-five minutes later the regular chief pilot, Tom Beekman, was saying, "I think it can be done. Here's what you have to do: Land at a nearby island with a longer runway and offload all but the amount of fuel you need to get there and back. Tell them to get the grass cut as short as possible — scalp it. Have them put up two windsocks, one at the threshold and one midway down the strip. I want you to be able to see what the wind is doing all the way in. Make sure they have runway end markers on both ends so that you can see clearly. Calculate a maximum weight figure for them and their luggage and tell them *no extras*. Leave the seats behind that are not needed. One kilo over and nobody flies. Got all that?"

"Yeah."

"Go for it, Paul, you'll make it."

I hung up the phone and sat there for a minute thinking: *What happened to No?*

*****

The sun doesn't really rise on the equator. Dawn doesn't fade into day with the slow grace of a Midwestern American morning. One moment the light is grey, and the next that brilliant, blistering orb rules the sky. I launched into it at 7:32 AM and turned north as it took dominion over the cobalt blue of the south Pacific. *Here we go.*

Having offloaded all the fuel I would not need, making the Aztec lighter than I had ever flown it, I was now on the business end of this whole deal, looking at the windsocks resting limply on their poles, studying the runway markers, and feeling the distance from one end of the runway to the other. "Boy that looks short," I said aloud to myself. But the numbers were right and the airplane, with so little fuel in it, felt different under me, much more agile and eager to respond. I made the turn on to final approach, added the last notch of flaps, and nailed the approach speed at sixty-three knots.

"Committed to land!" I called out loud. There was no bailing out now. The trees flew by on either side as I slowed the plane to the over-the-fence speed of fifty. The threshold rushed up at me. At the last moment I pulled the throttles back and flared onto the touchdown point. The main wheels thumped into the gravel with surefooted ease, and the nose came down with plenty of room to spare. Perfect!

As the speed fell off and the airplane rolled toward the end of the runway, I was already thinking about the departure. *OK, we need to get a bunch of guys out here to push the plane up to the end of the runway. I want all the room I can get for the takeoff roll.*

The missionary listened politely as I told him what I wanted, but before he complied he said, "Paul, I want you to meet some men." The whole village, about three hundred people, stood there as he introduced seven men. "These men are the elders of the church here, the leaders of the people. They have all been praying for you since you and I got off the radio. They prayed for your talk with the chief pilot."

I smiled inside. *Now I know why I'm here*, I thought, but I didn't say it out loud.

"These men have a song they'd like to sing for you, OK?"

"OK."

Indonesian music will never make the Top 40 in America, but when these men started to chant and stomp (they never sing without dancing), something chimed within me. I leaned back against the wing and listened. They were singing for all they were worth.

My friend translated when they finished, "Their song has four stanzas," he said. "Praise God the answer was yes! Praise God the answer was yes! The Chief pilot answered yes!" I smiled.

"Thank God he landed safely! Thank God he landed safely! Thank God the pilot landed safely!" He translated. "That's the second verse."

A great sense of peace settled over me then. I could sense that this was more than just a ceremony. God was at work in these people as they saw him answer their prayers. Their faith was being strengthened, as was mine.

"Please God, let them fly away safely! Please God, let them fly away safely! We will praise you even more!" That was the third stanza. I just kept smiling and watching.

The last one is the one that got me. It struck a tone in my soul that resonated all the way back to the day I was twelve years old and raised my hand to serve as a missionary. "May Mr. Pilot follow you all of his days! May Mr. Pilot follow you all of his days! May Mr. Pilot follow you all of his days!"

For a moment all the miles and the risks accumulated in the journey to serve God as a Mission Aviator came rushing back into conscious thought. And every one felt worth it. The anxiety of the last twenty-four hours fell away and the joy of serving these folks filled my soul. I clapped my hands and shouted, "Thank you! Thank you for praying for me!"

Then the men gathered round, pushed the airplane back to the very edge of the runway, helped us load it up, and we flew away. As the Aztec roared into the morning sky I thought, *I'm so glad I didn't say no!*

*****

Checklist:

✓ When was the last time you felt like God was asking you to push your personal margins?

✓ How have the prayers of others changed the course of your life?

Papuan women, truly "the least of these."

6

THE LAST SHALL BE FIRST

Papua, Indonesia

Women are dead last in the Papuan pecking order. A dog has a better life than a woman in Papuan culture. I was not aware of that truth until a flight that I made late in my career as a Mission Pilot.

As I was trying to get my passengers to load, they seemed hesitant. I couldn't figure out why. Finally, the translator enlightened me, "These folks are a bit scared. They don't want to go with you."

"Why? What's wrong?"

"They say that last time you were kind of cowboying around, rocking the wings and stuff, and they're just nervous about going with you."

I couldn't speak their tribal language, so I had to explain to them via the translator, "I do not fly that way. That was not me." And our pilots never fly that way. But to these folks all the white pilots look alike. If Jimmy Carter walked up to the plane they'd say, "Yeah, it was him! He was the one rocking the plane."

"No, they say it was definitely you."

"OK." I thought to myself, *just take it on the chin. You aren't going to convince them otherwise.* "Tell them I'll be real smooth, real careful."

Eventually, my passengers, a man, his wife, and an infant, along with the family's two small dogs, relented and clambered up into the plane.

It's a two hour flight from where we were back to Sentani, and I wanted to be sure they were happy with my flying, so about halfway into the trip I took a quick glance over my shoulder to see how they were doing. My eyes bulged as I stifled a gasp. *Whoa! Geez Louise, she's nursing!*

You might think that this is no big deal, that I should even expect this in a developing culture. Even Western women do that all the time nowadays. Some even breastfeed during church. They make special clothes for it right?

33

But this woman wasn't nursing her *baby*. Her baby was on her lap and she had a *dog* on each breast. She was nursing the dogs! I couldn't believe it. I was stunned!

How does this kind of thing happen to a woman? I come from a home and community that values women. I learned about the suffragettes and women's rights from grade school on. More important is the way that many of us grew up. My dad always modeled respect for my mom. It's a clear Biblical teaching. "Husbands love your wives as Christ loved the Church and gave himself up for her," said The Apostle Paul. "Show her honor as a fellow heir of the grace of life," echoed the Apostle Peter. Not all American men, or even American Christian men, follow those commands, but the values they stand for have informed American life from the beginning.

Not so in Papuan culture. From early childhood, every woman is told that she is less valuable than a dog. In the Papuan mountains, where subsistence farming and hunting is all they have to survive, a dog can get you a pig because a dog can hunt. A woman can't get you a pig, so the dog is more valuable. Men have all the power; women have nothing. Women are dead last in their value system.

In another village called Dau, a new territory for us and an undeveloped location where I had been flown in by helicopter, they were trying to build an airstrip. I was out there to check on their progress. I was totally focused on the land and how it lays and analyzing the angles and such – completely consumed with the task – not paying any attention to what was behind me, when suddenly I heard this blood curdling, animalistic scream. All I could think was *I'm dead. I'm about to be speared or shot with an arrow and I'm dead!*

I hit the dirt and zigzagged on my hands and knees away from this scream as fast as I could crawl, expecting any minute to feel the spear pinning me to the ground. About twenty-five feet away from the noise, I took a quick look over my shoulder and saw that it was a woman with a child.

Why was she screaming? Try to put yourself in her position. The Papuans are never more than about five feet tall and very dark skinned. She was maybe a little over four feet. I'm a six foot Scandinavian blonde wearing a white shirt and looking like nothing she's ever seen. All of her experience told her that I am either a wife stealer, which is bad for her and her baby, or I'm a spirit, which might be worse. She had no bow and arrow, no spear, and wouldn't know how to use it if she did. All she knew was that she was about to be a victim. End of story. She had no power, ever. She was always the one to suffer, always the victim. Papuan women can be disposed of. Papuan women, before the Bible is received, have a horrible life.

This state of affairs has bred helplessness in the hearts of Papuan women. They are used to living this way, existing at the bottom of the pecking order. They don't fight or question their position. They have no voice, and they don't expect one. The suicide rate for Papuan women is sixty percent. By their own volition they jump in the river and die. However, when the Bible comes to them in their mother tongue, when the Gospel of our Lord and Savior Jesus Christ is accepted by these people groups, that attitude changes. They are transformed by the saving power of Christ, and the dignity and value of every person is elevated. But the reason for the transformation is often surprising to a Westerner.

The most shocking thing about the New Testament for the Papuans is not Jesus' command to love your enemies, or even his rising from the dead and ascending into Heaven, which happens at the end of Matthew's twenty-eighth chapter. The most shocking thing for

Papuans is at the *beginning* of Matthew twenty-eight. What's at the beginning of Matthew twenty-eight? The discovery of the empty tomb. And who gets the news first? Who is the first one to find out that Jesus had risen? A woman!

When the Papuan men first hear this they're amazed. Their response is something like, "You've got to be kidding me! He gave that privilege to these things that are less than dogs? What is this? There must be something's wrong with *us*! It's not the women." When the story of Jesus is finally heard in their own heart language, the status of women soars.

Missionaries often hear complaints from anthropologists and others that people like the Papuans live in an ideal, undisturbed world, that we should respect their culture and leave them alone, and especially that we should not encourage them to change their religion. Yet how can anyone see this kind of suffering and abuse and not wish for it to change? Even so, we can't change it. And we don't ask them to exchange their religion for ours. Only the Gospel can transform these situations. We simply make the Bible available to them in their heart language.

The message of Jesus, when they can read it and begin to understand and accept it, changes their values. It changes these women's lives forever. It gives them a life they never had. Of course life is not perfect after the Gospel arrives; no culture is ever perfect. But the suicide rate among women drops to thirteen percent, because men begin to have a higher regard for women, and because women begin to have hope.

*****

Checklist:

✓   What shaped your attitude about the women in your life?

✓   How does the resurrection story – the fact that Jesus's first post resurrection appearance was to women – affect your attitude about women?

Miss an approach speed here and the results won't be pretty. Photo credit: Dane Skelton.

7

TRUST GOD AND KEEP YOUR POWDER DRY

Papua, Indonesia

"*Too slow! Too slow!* I said to myself. *You're gonna stall and crash before you reach the biggest airport in Papua! Get some power on this thing now!*

Mountain flying in Papua, Indonesia, is high performance flying. It isn't high performance because our planes are fast. They aren't. It isn't because we're doing aerobatics or stunt show work. We're not. It's high performance because Papua is the deadliest aviation environment in the world. The island claims at least half a dozen planes every year.

The threat is multifaceted and complex. The mountains produce their own weather systems, and they are unpredictable and often violent. The planes are almost always loaded to maximum weight and operated at high altitudes, a dangerous combination. The peaks of the mountains can top out over fourteen thousand feet. However, we don't usually fly that high, landing instead on short runways at six, or seven or even twenty percent grades at six thousand or seven or eight thousand feet above sea level to

Position Report - New Operators

Lots of aviation going on over here. New operators. Papua has a boom town/state mentality. Last month an experienced guy that used to fly for another mission flew into a mountain with a crew of 3 plus 9 passengers.

Three new operators on the block and 2 of the 3 are really scary at the first look. Like: "Hey Buddy, you know a thing or two about aviation, you just come on down here and fly this 19 passenger job into Okbob." Yikes! It is not if, but when something bad will happen.

All for now.

Pilot Paul in Papua

serve our clients. We have to navigate around and through the mountains, up valleys and down rivers that can fill up with weather and trap an unprepared pilot in minutes. The heat and tropical humidity play havoc with density altitude which is complicated, but basically means that an airplane's ability to climb is degraded due to thin air and can change dramatically from one day to the next. Then there is the trackless jungle. Drop your airplane into that endless canopy of green, and even if you survive the crash it is doubtful that anyone will ever find you. The jungle simply swallows you up. Every year the Mission Aviators based in Sentani are called out to do search and rescue (SAR) for aircraft lost in the jungle. Some are never found.

Our planes are specially designed and/or modified to operate in this environment, to take off and land at low speeds carrying heavy loads at high altitudes. They're called STOL airplanes for "Short Takeoff and Landing." In addition, our pilots are specially trained and our procedures have been carefully developed such that over the last sixty years, our organization has one of the best safety records in the world for what we do. Ultimately we know that our safety is in the hands of God, but we do our best not to test him on it. In the words of an old Civil War soldier, we trust God, but we keep our powder dry.

Just how much I was going to have to depend on God as a Mission Pilot came vividly to life during my first term in Papua. I was based a little over an hour west of Sentani, a bustling town of about fifteen thousand people that grew up around an airport initially built by Dutch colonists, expanded by the Japanese during World War II, and then taken over by General Douglas MacArthur on his island-hopping campaign against the Empire of the Sun. The airport is huge by Papuan standards, with a ten thousand foot long runway that can host big commercial jets like Boeing 737s, as well as our small planes. Many mission organizations are based there.

I launched one morning in the Helio Courier, a single engine STOL workhorse of an airplane, on a routine run to Maki to drop off supplies for a translator. Maki sits at the end of an incredibly steep, railroad-narrow, and stubby-short canyon that draws to a point on the far end. The Maki airstrip is carved into the side of one of the mountains, just above a river. It's only about an hour and five minutes from base, but it's the third scariest place we fly to from Sentani.

Procedure called for a high pass over the airstrip to check for obstructions, backtracking to the open end of the valley, checking the airspeed and altimeter just before entering this box canyon, and then a careful descent down the valley between the ridges. The trick is to get all the numbers right—airspeed, altitude, and descent rate—as you fly to the end of the box and land before you run out of room. Do it right and it is a thing of beauty. Get one of those three wrong, especially the airspeed, and end up in the river.

I scanned all three instruments every few seconds as I made the descent and got it right, feeling very satisfied with myself as I touched down. I made the supply drop, picked up a couple of passengers who needed to go to town, and roared away again for Sentani. *Nothing to it*, I thought. A smug grin spread across my face.

Everything seemed normal on the flight back to Sentani until I got into the pattern to land. Pilots fly the same pattern the world over. It's essentially one half of a rectangle flown with a constant rate of descent concluding on the ground. Airplanes are designed to be flown at a certain speed in this pattern. The Helio's initial pattern speed was 80 knots, or about 92 mph.

We were in the pattern and the airspeed indicator showed 80, but something didn't feel right. I tried to shake it off. *C'mon Westlund! What's the matter with you? Just fly the airplane!* I turned on the base leg, and still something wasn't right. The airspeed indicator showed 80 knots. I had just staked my life on its accuracy two hours ago in that canyon. But the airplane didn't *feel* right, the wind noise didn't *sound* right, the trees passing beneath us didn't *look* right. We were going too slow. *Too slow! Forget the airspeed indicator! You've got ten thousand feet of runway, not one thousand! Get some more speed on this thing now! Just use what you need and get down!*

I did. I got it on the ground and hauled it to a stop, a much longer landing rollout than usual. Then I looked again at the instruments. The airspeed indicator still read 80 knots, frozen in place. *If that had happened on the way into Maki*, I shuddered.

I unloaded my passengers and cargo and made a report on the problem and went home, thanking God all the way.

*****

Later on, when we inspected the plane, we found that the pitot system was clogged. The pitot system is made up of a small tube mounted on the leading edge of the wing with air lines flowing to the cockpit instruments. The instruments use the difference between the pressure in that system and the static air pressure system to calculate speed. Water had somehow gotten into it and stayed, even though the system had a drain and we covered it at night. After that incident, we equipped the fleet with permanent pitot covers that pivot open only when the plane is moving through air.

One of the reasons that I became a Mission Pilot is that I like being in situations where I am totally dependent on God. But that day I learned how totally dependent on him I really am. I also learned to keep my pitot system dry!

Checklist:

✓ What situations in your life have revealed your dependence on God?

✓ What changes have you made in "procedures" in order to minimize risk?

Heli-Mission can go where we can't.

8

PETER AND THE DEATH ADDER

Papua, Indonesia

Peter DeVries was trying very hard not to die, but the five Korawai men sitting on his front porch knew that was what he was going to do. They had come to say goodbye to the strange white man. That's what they always did when someone had been bitten by *The Snake*, say goodbye to the man who was about to die. They could tell that he was strong because he had come up from the river when the sun was still high overhead. Now it was near the horizon. It could not be long. They kept stealing grim glances at his face, watching for his eyes to droop and slowly, slowly close, never to open again.

The Snake is the Acanthopis, the Papuan Death Adder. The same snake is also found in Australia. Usually it's the geography that kills people here, the tropical diseases and isolation. But sometimes *The Snake* gets them.

Peter and his wife Maaike, Wycliffe Bible Translators, work among the Korawai people on the south coast of Papua, Indonesia.

The Korawai live in houses built high off the ground for safety from enemies as well as the Death Adder. The tree house construction is a bit different than what you or I would think. The area for the house has to have six or eight large trees. They cut down all the small trees and cut the large trees at the level they want for the floor of the house. Then they tie the trees together with jungle vines, using logs as rafters, creating a floor thirty feet in the air. The walls and roof are all made from what is right at hand: smaller trees, vines, and leaves for roofs. It is finished off with a three foot by three foot mud box in the center for a fire pit.

No adversary in his right mind would attack the bow-and-arrow-wielding Korawai in his high-perched home, and Death Adders don't climb trees.

> **Position Report - Worth It**
>
> Should have been home for lunch. Barely made it home for dinner.
>
> Rain delay, but did get translator's supplies to OMB. Rain and cloud delay, but did bring more translator supplies to OKB. Fog rolled in while unloading and had to wait 1 and 1/2 hours to take off for another village to fly mission carpenters back to town. All the holding and waiting and needing to go to other airports to wait meant I was getting low on fuel. The next question was: where is the weather good enough and do I have enough fuel stored there to get home?
>
> But one of my passengers today makes it worth it all. He is a former cannibal. But God's Word changed all that. Now he is a pastor and Bible teacher. He is a changed man.
>
> Pilot Paul in Papua

This snake, however, had caught Peter on the ground and unaware, but not unprepared. Unlike the Western tourist on a different island who had, a few years before, been struck by the Adder, Peter did not run back to the canoe that had carried him to a village downstream, paddle upstream, and run from the river back to camp yelling for help. That poor lady had died before the sun went down. Peter is an MK, a missionary kid who grew up in that part of the world. He knew from childhood that the one thing you don't want to do after a snake bite is run for help. Running just makes the heart pump faster, moving the poison from the bite to the vital organs in minutes instead of hours. Peter didn't run. As quickly as possible, he and a man named Aaron, along with his fiancée Rachel, young visitors investigating possible locations for doctoral research, immobilized his leg and, using their shirts as an improvised tourniquet, wrapped it tight just below the knee. With blood flow to the heart cinched off, they persuaded the local Korawai to help Aaron carry him back down to the canoe and paddle him back up stream to his village.

Unfortunately, the people in his own village of Siniburu weren't so easily persuaded. Some of them didn't like these white people, didn't trust them. Some had even tried to run them off.

"Why is your leg bandaged, Peter?" they asked.

"I've been bitten by the snake. I need you to carry me up to my house. Will you do that?"

The people near the stream just looked at him. Life in the jungle is hard, and the Korawai, like many of the people in that region, do not wish to be associated with bad events in other men's lives. It carries a bad omen. Blame might be shared. Besides, why sweat for a dead white man? They knew death would take him soon. That thinking makes no sense to Westerners, but the Korawai have yet to hear the story of the Good Samaritan.

It took some effort, but finally Peter and Maaike persuaded a few to help. They lifted him up on their shoulders and carried him up the steep hill to his porch. Maaike got a Wycliffe doctor on the satellite phone. Shortly, the five elders arrived to pay their last respects and say goodbye. Two went home when the sun went down, but the other three stayed. *Surely*, they thought, *he would not last the night.*

I was unaware of all this while I was flight planning and loading the plane for a simple out-and-back flight to drop off two groups of Mother Tongue Translators (MTT), a term for people from a local language group that are doing the Bible translation, in their various villages. (MTTs make it possible for us to do multiple translations at the same time, moving us faster toward the goal of starting Bible translations in all of the yet-to-be-translated languages by 2025). These MTT's had been to town to attend a workshop to gain more experience and more tools to speed the work of getting the Bible into their language groups. They were anxious to get home after the business of town. After dropping them off, I would pick up Rachel and Aaron Yanirumah and be back home for lunch. At least that was the plan.

I loaded the MTTs and took off, but on the way out I learned that the south coast was covered with thick fog. I knew that I'd have to kill a bunch of time waiting for the fog to burn off. I started asking the villagers if they had goods to sell in Wamena, the largest city on earth accessible only by air. They are able to get a much better price in Wamena for pigs and sago and bananas and peanuts than in their own village. Getting a higher price for their goods enables them to pay school fees for their children and improves their quality of life with goods and medicine from the big city.

From Wamena I fueled up and started to look for loading on my way down to Yanirumah. That's when the call from the doctor came over the radio:

"Peter Jan DeVries has been bitten by a Death Adder and is going by helicopter to Dekai." Dekai, or DEK as we sometimes call it, is about thirty minutes southeast of Wamena, a place where we store fuel for days like this one when plans change en route. "You need to meet up with the helicopter in DEK and fly Peter directly to the hospital in Timika."

People see me as a brave person to fly out here, but I get to go home most nights. You need a special kind of brave to live out in the jungle, send your husband to the hospital with a snake bite, and keep moving on for the sake of the Good News, especially when the people you work with don't understand what you are doing and cannot appreciate the sacrifice you are making. That's the kind of people Bible Translators are. That's what Maaike DeVries did.

The rapid thop thop thop of the helicopter broke the sweltering stuffiness of the midday air. Maaike, who had been straining her ears for it for over an hour, heard it first. Peter, who had slept sitting up to get gravity's assistance in keeping the poison contained in his leg and away from his heart, watched it curl in on approach and lightly touch down. His Korawai friends, who had watched him with increasing amazement through the night, wordlessly picked him up and carried him to the thrumming machine. Then he called his four children to his side.

"Children, Daddy is going to be ok. I am going to make sure I will be ok. Good-bye. Good-bye! Take care of your mother!"

Aaron and Rachel helped the pilot load their gear and then jumped in with Peter. They were off for DEK where I waited in the Yajasi airplane.

My home base had given me the flight time data and estimated fuel needed for the trip. Even so, as a bush pilot you learn to double check everything, double check so that you are *never* guessing. I was skeptical that something was amiss with the data. So with a bit of extra time in DEK, I filled my fuel tanks to give us more options.

Visible heat waves scattered as the chopper touched down on the hot black tarmac at DEK, which was suddenly a beehive of activity. With the engine still running and the blades spinning, the pilot and nurse and a helper carried Peter to my plane. Rachel, who had climbed into the helicopter barefoot, and Aaron piled out and suddenly didn't know what to do.

"Ouch! Give me one of your sandals quick!" she cried. Aaron slipped one off and slid it over to her. Now they were both hopping around on one foot, fifteen feet from the spinning tail rotor, trying to figure out what to do.

"We need to get moving!" I shouted above the roar of the engine and whirling death just fifteen feet away. Their hopping around and imbalance so close to the tail rotor was giving me chills even on the broiling tarmac. "Do you guys want to ride the chopper to Wamena and try to pick up a flight to Sentani from there? Or go with Peter and me to Timika and try to make it back to Sentani that way?" I yelled.

It sounds simple until you factor in the unpredictable weather and the mountains we had yet to cross. They could easily end up spending another night in the jungle and disrupt other carefully laid and already paid for travel plans.

Aaron stood like a Whooping Crane under the noisy rotor and yelled to Rachel, "What do you want to do, honey?"

It's funny to watch the newly married or the recently engaged try to avoid disagreement. Rachel had grown up on the field and knew the vagaries of travel in the developing world. Yet she deferred to Aaron, who was uncertain at best. "I think you should decide!"

The confusion, the noise from the chopper, the heat, the gravity of the medical situation, their bare feet, and proximity to that tail rotor made my gut churn. *Not good. Not good!* I thought.

Pilots don't always make the right decisions, but we do know how to make decisions quickly.

"OK! OK!" I said. "You can't know what will happen either way. Just take your chances with me."

Now I needed to get their bags out of the helicopter and into my airplane. The engine was still running and the tail rotor, which will kill you much faster than the Death Adder, whirred away just feet from our heads. I shouted to them, "Don't move!" and glanced over to the cargo hold of the helicopter. I looked back at them and repeated, "don't move." I opened the latch and looked back at them. I didn't want to take my eyes off of them, but I had to get their gear. I grabbed one bag and shot another glance at them, then another bag and turned toward them again.

"Don't move!" I commanded. I saw some gloves in the cargo hold and threw them on the ground near them to give the pair something to put their balancing hot feet on. Now at least they weren't dancing.

In the last bag was a pair of soggy sneakers. They both grabbed at them wanting the wet shoes to give their burning feet some relief. I straightened up from the cargo hold but still kept my head down under the chopper's main rotor. Trying to keep my wits about me, we grabbed their bags, and I slowly led them away from the death-dealing tail rotor toward the Wycliffe plane. Once outside the danger area, I turned and motioned *all clear* to the chopper pilot who powered up and slowly, like some huge humming bird, levitated a few feet off the ground, and flew away.

Rachel is an MK. She is our daughter's age and was often in our house growing up. She is very comfortable around me. "I need to go potty!" she said.

"Now?" I asked.

She nodded vigorously. I've learned that you don't say no to a woman like that. You just give her options.

"OK! You have a choice: the ditch or the deep grass. Run there and run back as fast as you can, we need to get moving."

She was back in a flash, and we were off for Timika.

Now it was my turn to watch the patient. Like clockwork I kept looking back at Peter every five minutes to see if he was breathing ok and to see if he was going to sleep or if his eyes lids were starting to sag.

We touched down in Timika with Peter no worse off than when he was carried to the plane. With a great sense of relief I helped carry him to the ambulance where the driver and his aid took over. The sight of the ambulance brought a crowd of onlookers. Some security men, aircraft loaders, and airport baggage handlers, and even another pilot came over to the plane to see what was going on. One asked, "What's was wrong with the guy with the bandaged leg? Did he fall out of a tree?"

"No," I explained. "He was bitten by *The Snake*, the kind where you get ready to die. And confess your sins to Jesus and prepare for the next life."

I love opportunities to testify like that because you never know what's going to happen. Most of the white shirted, epaulets-wearing pilots they hear only brag about themselves, especially about their relationships with women. One Papuan ground crewman was so happy to hear a pilot talking about trusting in Almighty God that he jumped out of the group and gave me a bear hug.

With Rachel and Aaron running back from a real bathroom, I rechecked my fuel and tied down their bags and closed the doors. We were off again, after eleven minutes on the ground and two hours of fighting weather and we *might* make it home.

At thirteen thousand feet I slipped the oxygen mask on, took a look at my two passengers and grinned. They were fast asleep. I flew as smooth as I could so they would not notice the effects of the altitude. At fifteen thousand feet I would need to give them oxygen, but we do not have that equipment for passengers. We would be forced to turn around if I had to go higher. Halfway across the high mountains there was a big rain cell right on the route, but I was able to leave the normal route and stay in the clear at thirteen thousand feet until out of the mountains. I was glad that I had loaded the extra fuel.

Two days later Peter had clearance from the hospital to go home. I was able to take him back to DEK to meet up with the helicopter. We talked a bit on the ride back.

"Paul, it is amazing what God has done in the Korawai people. When we first arrived everyone was very harsh. No one trusted us. Some even tried to force us to leave. Now fifty percent of them are our close friends and about half of that number is following the Word of God."

*****

Checklist:

✓ What do you think about people who risk their lives for the kingdom of God?

✓ Someone has said, "If there is nothing you would die for, you don't have much to live for." Is there anything that you would risk your life for? If so what is it, and why?

The Papuans became my good friends.

9

FINDING A FRIEND IN
A FOREIGN LAND

Ambon Island, Maluku Island Chain, Indonesia

My favorite story from the Civil War is about a very clever, very successful spy. His effectiveness was based not on his cloak and dagger skills, but on his ability to befriend his enemies. He made friends with enemy soldiers by meeting their needs—a little salt here or some socks there or a letter forwarded to a wife. When he was finally discovered to be a spy and sentenced to be shot by the men he had befriended, they didn't have the heart to do it. So they let him go.

I remember reading that story as a boy and thinking, *I like that. I just want to be a friend to everyone I meet.* And that's what I do. I'm not interested in spying. I go out of my way to let people know that I care about them. That's how Pak Markus and I became friends. (Pak is Indonesian for *Mr.*). Neither of us had a clue about the adventures that lay before us; we were just friends. But I've learned something powerful over the years: Never underestimate what God can do when we love others the way Jesus has loved us.

> **Position Report - Rats for Dinner**
>
> LaVonne has a group of bachelors over for supper on Tuesday nights. One young man is a missionary named Peter. Last time I picked him up in the village, he offered me some crackers. They were chewed on a bit. "What is this?" I asked.
> "Oh, a rat got in my food!"
> Well, this last time out in the village, he got so low on food that he was eating rat! He really appreciates LaVonne's hospitality.
>
> Pilot Paul in Papua

I had just started flying in Maluku, a small group of islands known for their spices, on the eastern end of the Indonesian archipelago. Pak Markus was from a village in one of the towns I served, a successful businessman whose two children, a girl, Sirong and a boy, Lutut, were old enough to go to school. Like any parents, Pak and Ibu (Mrs.) Markus wanted the best education possible for their kids. Markus' success as a businessman with shipping and jewel interests made it possible for him to move his family from his small town to the large town of Ambon and to use air travel to stay in touch with his business on his home island. Though other carriers operated in and out of his island, he was so impressed with the professionalism and safety record of YAJASI, the group I flew for, that he wouldn't fly with any other.

YAJASI is an Indonesian acronym that stands for *The Aviation Foundation Serving Bible Translation*. It is an Indonesian organization that partners with Wycliffe in the work of Bible Translation. Its primary mission is to provide safe, reliable transportation for translation teams in Papua and the surrounding islands. Because aviation is expensive, YAJASI, as well as other mission aviation organizations, also flies commercial and government clients to defray the costs of air travel for the missionaries who depend on it.

Pak Markus was one of those customers. Unlike the others, Markus was interested in aviation and wanted to be my friend and showed it in tangible ways. He recommended friends and business contacts to our service. He watched the schedule for flights out to his island, coordinating his trips home when he knew we were headed that way. Though I always take a lunch box when I fly, I never needed it when I flew to Markus' island. He made sure one of his employees met me with hot food and cold drinks. That's just the kind of man he is—a good friend.

Pak Markus dropped by the hangar a few months after his first flight with me and said, "Paul, tell me about this airplane. Why does YAJASI use it instead of some of the others?" And we launched into a long discussion about the virtues and limits of the Piper Aztec I was then flying. In the following weeks, Markus became a regular visitor to the hangar. We had a lot of talks like that and found we enjoyed each other's company. We trusted each other. He even came to my son's first birthday party.

On a Saturday a little over a year later, I took our two-year-old son Mark out to the hangar to show him Daddy's plane and give LaVonne a break from parenting. Markus pulled in a few minutes after we arrived.

"Markie, you remember Pak Markus. Can you say hi?"

"Hi, Pak Markus!"

"Hello, Mark." Markus smiled and got down on one knee. "Are you helping Dada today?"

"Yes!"

The hangar phone rang. "Hey Pak Markus, I need to answer that phone, can you watch the little guy a bit?"

"Sure."

"Don't let him crank up the airplane." I grinned.

He chuckled, "We won't take off without you, will we, Markie?"

And Mark was ok with that. It told me a lot about the spirit of this man that my two-year-old was comfortable with him. I picked up the jangling phone.

"Paul, this is Yuliar." The voice sounded urgent.

"Oh hi, Yuliar, what can I do for you?"

"Paul, we have a very sick woman here. Malaria, we think. Can you make a flight to us today and take her to the hospital?"

I looked at my watch and did some quick math on time and distance and fuel.

"Yeah, I can do that," I said. "How about two hours from now?" But then I remembered Mark. I couldn't make it in two hours if I had to drive the forty minute round trip necessary to get him home and get me back to the hangar. "Hey wait a minute. I gotta check something."

Yuliar held the line while I walked over and explained the situation to Pak Markus.

"No problem, Paul. But don't you think we should ask Mark?"

"Oh yeah!" I knelt down by Mark and spoke gently to him. "Hey Markie, you think you could ride home with Pak Markus? Daddy's got to go help somebody."

"Sure! Let's go for a ride!"

It's one thing to make a business acquaintance in a hangar on a remote island in the South Pacific. It's quite another to trust him with the safety of your own son. I knew I could trust Markus. Amazingly, so did little Mark. I buckled my son into Markus' car, kissed him goodbye, and began preparing the plane. Silently I thanked God for a new friend. I had no idea how important that friendship would be to me later on or how important it would be to Markus, when crisis struck.

*****

Checklist:

✓ What is your attitude about building friendships?

✓ Who is your most important friend on this earth and how did you meet him or her?

I could land on the beach, but the tide would take the airplane.
Photo credit: Yay photos / Friday.

10

WOUNDED SPARROW

Maluku Islands, Indonesia

Few things raise a pilot's pulse like a dead engine. Mine was racing. One of the engines on my Aztec had just gone silent, and I wasn't too sure about the other one. As the altimeter unwound rapidly through four thousand feet, I reached for the life jackets just behind us and handed one to my friend. "Put this on, Markus. We're a single engine airplane now out over the big water."

I was trying to stay nonchalant, but Markus could see the strain on my face. He reached over and lightly touched my arm. "Are we going to make it my friend?"

"Yes."

Markus didn't let go, instead, he put his fingers on my wrist. Checking someone's pulse is the jungle's lie detector. After a minute or two he let go, satisfied that I was shooting straight with him.

Position Report - Return to Base

"Aircraft UCF return to base."

About to take off on one mission and the call came through to change plans. Unload the plane and go and rescue a sick Bible Translator. Dave Briley puts up with bouts of malaria in order to get God's Word into the Bauzi language.

Pray for Dave. He was so sick today I don't think he knew who picked him up.

Pilot Paul in Papua

My pulse didn't matter at the moment. The altimeter did, and it was still unwinding like a sick clock. I mentally reviewed engine out ditching procedures in the Aztec. As we passed through two thousand feet, I started thinking not just about keeping the airplane airborne, but about surviving, period. Markus asked again, "Are we going to make it?"

I hoped so, but I was by no means certain. The day had started off with much more promise.

The hangar phone had rung early that morning and my friend was on the other end. "Hello, Pilot Paul!"

"Markus! Hello, my friend!"

"I dropped by the airport yesterday afternoon and saw that you are making a run down to my home island today. Do you have room for me? I need to check on things there."

Pak Markus is a skillful business man, intuitive and quick to realize when one market is about to plateau and another to emerge. He had diversified into many businesses early in his career. When one business hit a snag, he never missed a beat, ramping up activity in a different area to compensate for slower trade elsewhere. That approach required a lot of travel between various islands in the huge Indonesian archipelago. Since YAJASI had only one plane in his home area, I became his de facto chief pilot, his go-to guy for air travel. The trip from my base to his home island took two and one half hours. He often made the trip twice a week, so we spent a lot of time together in the air in the mid nineteen nineties, and the friendship grew.

"In fact I do, Markus. I'm going down to pick up one of our translators. If you go, I won't have to fly empty."

"Excellent. I will see you soon."

Great, I thought. *I'll have a paying customer on the outbound leg and a missionary on the inbound.* Markus arrived a few minutes before I finished loading the plane. We buckled into the twin engined Piper Aztec that we used for over-water flights and launched into the bright blue morning sky.

About thirty minutes out, my mind began to wander. Once the course is set, the engines tuned to peak efficiency, and the airplane trimmed at cruising altitude, a pilot's workload lightens, and he has time to think. That's what I was doing on that April 11, five thousand feet above the ocean and two hours out of our destination—scanning my instruments, scanning the horizon, and thinking. At forty-two years of age with ten years on the field at that time, and thousands of hours in small piston-powered airplanes. I was re-evaluating my own horizons. I was thinking about the future. I was thinking about leaving the mission field.

That's when the number two engine yanked my thoughts back into the cockpit. Without audible warning and with all the gauges in the green, the engine just stopped, like flipping off a light switch. I went through the restart procedure, but I knew from the way it had quit that it was probably an ignition problem and would not restart. Instinctively I checked the Global Positioning System. Pak Markus and I were one and a half hours from a safe landing.

Training took over as I killed the autopilot, pushed the nose over into a shallow dive, chopped the fuel to the right engine, and feathered the prop. At that moment a vivid image popped into my mind: another Mission Aviator in a twin engine airplane operating in the Caribbean had lost an engine on takeoff. Instead of pushing the nose down to maintain enough airspeed over the wings to stay in control and splash down – the way Captain Sullenburger did to land his airliner in the Hudson – the pilot had kept the yoke back, fighting for altitude, yet losing critical airspeed. The wing with the dead engine stalled, the airplane rolled inverted, and the pilot and his son spun to their deaths. The one thing I had going for me was that I was already at cruising altitude when the engine quit.

All of my training and experience in Piper Aztecs told me I had two options: I could run the remaining engine at max power and try to maintain altitude. Or I could reduce power to ninety percent and descend to an altitude where the air was dense enough for the plane to maintain at least eighty-nine knots of airspeed, the minimum required to avoid the stall on one engine.

But how low was low enough? And would the remaining engine take the strain? The plane was loaded to its maximum weight. If I went by the book, I would operate it at full power and cruise at or above one thousand feet, but this was an older engine. I didn't want to take the chance that it would fly apart under the load. I put the left engine at ninety percent power and descended, number two hanging like a dead man on the airplane's right shoulder, creating drag where it had once produced thrust. I kept constant pressure on the left rudder pedal, working to keep the wounded bird straight and the sink rate manageable, and made a course change to the closest available airfield, still over an hour away. I later learned that, unlike the training airplane in the States, the Robertson STOL kit installed on that particular Aztec made it controllable down to seventy-nine knots, or ten knots slower. But that gap in my knowledge wouldn't be filled until later.

That's when Markus held my arm gently in his hand and once again asked, "Are we going to make it?"

"Yes." Satisfied once again, he let go. But he rechecked his seat belt and looked thoughtfully out at the cobalt blue water below.

We were at one thousand feet, then nine hundred, eight hundred. The needle slowed its counter clockwise circle as we sank through seven hundred fifty feet. Finally, at six hundred feet above the waves, low enough to read the name on a cargo ship we passed, the sturdy old Piper leveled out. We had been flying for over an hour then, burning fifteen more gallons of fuel, and thus lightening the load by about six pounds per gallon. The Aztec started to climb ever so slowly. A little thrill of triumph shot through me then. *We're gonna make it*, I said to myself with much more confidence.

Staying out of the water wasn't all I was thinking about. *If I get out of this alive*, I thought, *I'm going back to the States*.

To the young, serving God in the jungles or giving one's life to full-time ministry of any kind looks like a grand adventure. In your mid forties the perspective changes, even for missionaries. I could feel my body aging. Retirement was coming up on my horizon, and my nest egg was nowhere near the size of my friends' in the secular world. I loved what I was doing, serving "the least of these" with aviation and speeding the work of Bible translation. Nonetheless the strains of life on the field and the inherent danger of the kind of flying I was doing were taking a toll. My journey felt tougher than it had to be. And God seemed farther away than he was when I was young.

The altimeter showed seven hundred feet. A small island beach came into view. The tide was out. *I could put it down there*, I thought. *That beach is long enough, but the airplane will be a total loss as soon as the tide comes in.*

I pushed on another half hour or so, inching back up to one thousand feet as I did. The crash crew was ready. They'd heard my distress call, though I was convinced we wouldn't need them. We circled a few miles off of the island to let a rain squall clear the beautiful thirteen hundred meter long runway and set up for a straight line approach. I was feeling better about our chances every second, until I tried to drop the landing gear.

The Aztec's landing gear is hydraulically operated. Each engine drives a pump supplying the hydraulic system. On final approach, the pilot pushes down on a wheel-shaped lever below the center console, feels the familiar drag of the wheels interrupting the slip-stream, followed by the *thunk* of the gear locking into place. He then checks the panel for three green indicator lights telling him the gear is down and locked. The whole process takes about three seconds. I pushed the lever down and counted to three. I felt the drag, but no *thunk*. No green lights either.

The runway threshold loomed ahead. We were only two hundred feet off the deck and descending at five hundred feet per minute, or eight feet per second. Once the gear is partially down on an engine-out approach in a fully loaded Aztec, there is no go around option. We *had* to land. We had about twenty-five seconds before impact.

Low oil pressure! I thought. *Without the number two engine the pressure is too low, and the gear might not lock before touch down! Time to use up some of this beautiful runway!* I shoved the throttle forward on number one, bringing the RPMs up and with it the hydraulic pump speed. The pressure came up, and I felt that oh-so-satisfying *thunk!*

"Three greens gear down and locked," I said out loud. And then we were on the ground, taxiing to the ramp, rolling to a tie down, pulling the mixture back to idle cutoff, and watching the blades come to a stop. The deep whirring of decelerating gyros made a peaceful backdrop to an otherwise silent moment. I took a deep breath and let it out slowly.

"Good work, my friend," Markus smiled as he shook my hand. Seeing a mechanic approaching to help with the plane, he climbed out on the wing and as if we'd only had a flat tire on the side of road said, "You fellows figure this out and I'll go find us some lunch and we'll be on our way."

Once we had the upper cowling off of the number two engine, I leaned in to have a look at the dual magnetos, the source of ignition for the spark plugs. Sure enough, the drive gear for both mags was disengaged. The bolt that held it to the camshaft had backed off just enough to allow it to slip out.

When my friend got back with lunch I said, "We're not flying anywhere else today, Markus. I'm going to have to go get parts and come back later. Maybe you can catch a boat to your island."

"Where are you going to stay?"

"I don't know. I'll find something."

"No, no, my friend," he smiled. "I have family on this island. I will take the boat on to my destination; you will stay with them tonight."

It was a comfortable end to a harrowing day. I stretched out on the bed that Markus's family provided that night, pulled the mosquito netting across and made it secure, took a deep breath, and prayed.

"God, I thank you for getting us safely on the ground today, for the training that I have to know how to do a job like that. And if it's all the same to you, I'd rather not have to do it again. I've served you here with my whole heart and I'm willing to stay at it, but maybe it's time I went home? Please show me," I yawned. "Please ... show me," I repeated, and drifted off to sleep.

His answer would come six months later in a way that I could never have imagined.

The letter from my supporter came as a shock. I opened and read this question: "Paul, where were you and what were you doing at 1:30 AM Eastern Time on April 11?"

I worked out the fourteen-hour time differential and flashed back two months from the date on the letter to April 11. I knew exactly where I'd been—holding that airplane up on one engine over shark-infested ocean.

I put the letter in my lap and looked out the window. In my more honest moments, I knew what was driving my fantasies of returning to the States. It wasn't the money or the equipment or the strain of flying over trackless jungles and open water. What I really needed wasn't money or vacations or an expensive car. It was a touch from God. It came in that letter.

It read:

"Paul, as you know, I live alone. At 1:30 in the morning of April 11, I felt someone slap me on the side of my neck. I woke up immediately, and sat up in bed wondering 'what in the world?' but saw nothing. Just then I became intensely aware that you were in trouble over water, and I needed to pray for you. I prayed. I could not stop praying for an hour and a half. Paul, are you OK?"

I leaned back in my chair, gentle warmth filling my soul like sunshine on a spring morning. My eyes glazed over and began to fill with tears. At 1:30 AM Eastern time, I'd been studying that small island beach from six hundred feet above the sea, thinking about landing on it and leaving the plane to the surf.

Sometime later, I heard from a friend named Scott. Scott flew corporate jets for a big tool company in the States: Gulfstream G-IVs, King Airs, all turbine stuff with pressurized cabins, the latest avionics. These planes are the Lexuses of the air. "I don't want to steal you from the mission field, but if you are ready, I have been holding a jet job for you," he wrote.

A pilot usually has to have one thousand hours of airtime in turbine powered planes before a big outfit will consider him for such service. All of my time to that point was in small piston-powered planes. Scott was opening a huge door for me with great pay and benefits, one that didn't depend on thirty-year-old airplanes, short mountain airstrips, and dances with destiny above the waves. I knew what I had to do.

"Thanks, but no thanks." I said. "I cannot trade the prayers of God's people for the coolness of flying a jet and the money it would bring."

*****

It's funny how God works things out in our lives sometimes. On that day when I turned Scott down, I thought I'd never see the cockpit of a turbine powered aircraft. In 2006, in my twentieth year as a jungle pilot, I transitioned into the turbine powered Pilatus PC-6 Porter.

Checklist:

✓ What dreams have you said good-bye to, only to have them fulfilled years later?

✓ How have the prayers of others shaped your life?

PART TWO

OBSTACLES, ACCIDENTS, AND OPPORTUNITIES

An airfield was on the island that hadn't been used since WWII.
Photo credits: Yay photos / Iofoto

11

THE FLIGHT THAT NEVER HAPPENED

Ambon Island, Maluku Islands, Indonesia

The Tabers were in trouble. The bad news had come through on inter-island radio.

"Mark sounded very tired and worried," said the man who took the call. I knew Mark pretty well. He was not the worrying type.

"Kathy has malaria, and he is pretty sure one of his girls does too," he continued. "They need to get out of the village and to a doctor as soon as possible. He left a message for you to call him from the radio phone office this afternoon at 2:30."

Malaria. The word sent a shudder through me. Imagine having the flu: the fever, the chills, the bone-deep ache in all of your muscles and joints, the vomiting and fatigue. It lasts a few days and then with rest begins to fade. You think you're over it. So you get up and try to do normal things like make lunch or change the oil in the car. Then it hammers you again and lasts longer. The next time it fades you are weaker. You try to get up again, just to get a glass of water or take a shower.

> **Position Report - Four Steps Above Hell**
>
> What a life out here. Helping a man sell his pigs for his son's doctor bills, dealing with desperate people at a place that are pleading with me for a flight out.
>
> Dealing with people that are lying to me about weather and winds and putting me at risk to come to their place because they are in such need.
>
> Land at a place where a man begs to get on as the people might kill him there. Ask a passenger to get out to be picked up later and hear, "No please not me, this place is only four steps above hell."
>
> Pilot Paul in Papua

Then it returns and lasts for days. It is especially hard on children. You get the picture. Missionaries endure it as part of the job. Death or permanent brain damage can come agonizingly slowly without treatment.

We had to get them out. What do you do when lives are at stake but rescuing them might endanger your whole operation? That's the situation I faced that day. I was flying from Ambon Island back then, long before the jihad of 1999 that made it impossible for us to work there. Ambon is part of the Maluku Island chain, a little north and west of Papua. The Tabers were serving on one of the farthest outlying islands, painstakingly building up the relationships and the database they needed to continue the Bible translation. They were doing it mostly without air support.

From our base on Ambon, Mark and Kathy and their three small children had to buy rides on small watercraft, sometimes no more than a long outrigger canoe with an outboard motor, and island hop their way to their village. The trip could take nine days because there was no runway on their island or anywhere nearby. At least that's what I thought.

That wasn't the only problem. Even if the Tabers had an airport, I wasn't supposed to be flying.

"Paul, this guy Pak Milky is real trouble," Pak Bram my manager had said the day before as he walked out of our small office and into the hangar.

"What do you mean?" I looked up from the brake repair I was doing on our Piper Aztec.

"Well, I just got off the phone with him, and he's saying that a new tax has tacked on some extra fees to your flight license here and he can't release it until they are paid."

"How much?"

"One thousand four hundred dollars, and a round trip ticket to Manado."

I hit the ceiling. "Fourteen hundred dollars and a round trip ticket?"

"Yeah, and he says it needs to be cash, no receipts."

I looked back down at the disc brake and back up at Bram. "He wants a bribe, right?"

"Yeah, welcome to the Third World."

"Are we going to pay it?"

"Nope. We don't do bribes. It only asks for more."

"What'll we do?"

"We wait and we pray. Eventually something will break. He'll need us or he will need somebody else with some leverage and he'll stand down. Until then, you're grounded."

Not long after that, we got the call from the Tabers.

I managed to connect with Mark Taber a few hours later. "Paul, I don't think Kathy or Sheri could make that trip by boat. They are both very weak."

"What do you suggest, Mark? I don't know of any other way to get you guys out of there. Where would I pick you up? And besides, there's another issue you don't even know about. I am having trouble renewing my license to fly."

Mark never spoke to the second issue, but he did tell me something I didn't know.

"The local people tell me that there is a really long runway on a neighboring island called Moa. It's only about an hour away from us by boat. They say it has an old airfield on it. It must have been there since the war."

"Let me check my charts," I said. "I'll call you back in thirty minutes, OK?"

"I'll be waiting. Mark out."

Bram and I went back to the hangar and grabbed all of the navigation charts of the area we could find and poured over them looking for a runway, but nothing doing. There was no runway shown on any island near the Tabers, including Moa.

I reluctantly got back on the radio, "Ambon to Mark Taber. Mark do you read?"

"I'm here, Paul."

"Mark, we're not showing any airports on our charts. Are you sure about this?"

"Yes. We have it on good authority that there is a very long runway there. We think the Japanese built it, and the Americans never used it during the war. That's why it doesn't show up on any charts. It's hasn't been used since 1945 and has some craters and things growing in it, but it's very long and wide for one of our small bush airplanes," he explained.

Then he paused for a second or two, "Paul, Kathy, and Sheri are really sick. I'm very worried. Would you be willing to chance it?"

"Hang on for a bit, OK?"

"Yeah, OK."

I looked at Pak Bram, and he looked back at me with a furrowed brow. I knew I had to go, but if I crashed or even got a flat tire, I would never fly again in Indonesia.

"Go," he said, "I will take the responsibility. Just don't come back with so much as a scratch on that airplane."

We both knew we had to take the risk and get the Tabers out and then face the music if something bad happened.

"And when the Tabers are back here safe and sound," he added, "that flight will not go in the books; it will never have happened. You did not fly that day."

I smiled and got back on the radio, "Mark, how soon can you get there?"

"We can be there by nine tomorrow morning."

"OK. When you get there, build a smoky fire on the end of the runway with the fewest holes and obstructions. Got it?"

"Yes! Yes! I got it! We'll be there. And I'll make sure you can find us."

I took off the next morning with full fuel and flew my best-guess course to Moa, using Mark's island as a navigation waypoint. As I crossed his island, I descended to five hundred feet to make any smoke spiral more visible against the bright blue morning sky. Approaching Moa Island, I didn't see anything at first, just a patch of grey sand and next to it, white surf rising out of emerald water.

"Mark, I hear something," Kathy said. She was sitting in the shade of a palm tree while Mark looked for more wood.

"Me too, mom, I hear it too!" their daughter offered. Mark stepped out of the shade and held his hand over his eyes to block the glare. "There he is! There he is!" he pointed to the eastern sky.

Mark could see me about a mile out. They threw the thin green leaves they had been saving on the fire which offered up a thick white smoke trail.

There you are! Now let's take a look at this runway.

I banked slightly and eased the throttle back for a shallow descent down to three hundred feet, keeping the runway off to my left for a good look.

It's long! I thought. *Like, really long!* It looked to be more than three miles long and one quarter mile wide. It appeared to be a kind of grey sandy color and ran east to west along the southern coast of Moa. *And it's in really good shape! The Japanese must have launched bombers from here. Some craters on this end, but the other end, closer to that grove of trees looks ok. The hot prevailing winds from Northwest Australia must have kept anything from taking root down here. I'll shoot for touchdown at the middle.*

It felt strange to land on a runway that hadn't been used since 1945. I imagined Japanese Zeros and Betty bombers parked in revetments along the edges. I thought I could still make out the outlines of bunkers and the pole where a wind sock once flew as I glided in on approach. I touched down without incident and taxied down to where Mark and his family waited. They were putting out the signal fire, and as they did, the smoke drifted sideways from the on-shore winds.

"Thanks, Paul! Thanks for coming to get us! We don't know what we would have done."

"It is a privilege to serve you. And nice runway you found us here. Now let's get you all to the doctor."

A couple of weeks went by after that. I kept busy on the ground with maintenance on the aircraft, and Kathy and their little girl rested and recovered from confirmed cases of Malaria. Sure enough, Pak Milky came through with my license ... without the extra fees. I guess he just got tired of waiting.

*****

Later on, after I had been flying again for a while, I reported to the Aviation Authorities about the great condition of their airfield on southern Moa. They opened the airfield for use, which made it much easier to service the needs of all of the people in that area.

Kathy is one of those people who is pretty serious about life. She almost hates to use a phone. She does not do small talk, is eager for the singing to stop and the preaching to start in church. So the next time I saw her I talked about flying three pastors down to Moa for the day of a church dedication.

When I ran out of things to say about Moa and the church service, she looked me square in the eyes and said, "Paul, we're *so* glad that the government opened this runway. I'm happy to hear about that dedication service. And I have to tell you that I've never heard a sweeter sound than that day when I was so sick and heard you and your airplane coming to the rescue."

Checklist:

✓ What kinds of ethical dilemmas have you faced in your work?

✓ Read the story of David's escape from Saul in 1 Samuel 19:1-7. How does it inform your thinking about such difficulties?

Medical evacuation flights keep us very busy.

12

MYSTERY OF THE MISSING FUEL DRUMS

Papua, Indonesia

Airplanes only hold so much fuel. Mission Aviators spend about twenty-five percent of their time planning where they will get their next load of fuel and provisioning their outlying airstrips with extra drums of the precious liquid. These drums provide the gas to get us home on long days. A simple departure from the planned route to dodge a thunderstorm can mean an overnight stay in a jungle village to wait for a fuel delivery, a logistics complication in everyone's schedule.

One of our translators Mrs. Moxness and her kids needed to get back to town. I was on my way to pick them up, which is usually a three hour trip with a stop on the way. Her husband, Mike Moxness, would stay behind for awhile, continuing the translation work without his wife. The plan was to pick him up two weeks later and reunite him with his family in Sentani.

The Moxness' village Siriwo was one of my fuel depots, where I kept two empty fifty-five gallon drums in a locked shed. Since the village is so far from my base, I could fill all four wing tanks in Sentani, off load some of the avgas in Siriwo, and two weeks later use that fuel I had stored to get me and Mr. Moxness home. At least that was the plan.

Siriwo is one of those "extra prayer, extra care" runways. It is steeply sloped, almost always has a tailwind, and is only three hundred and seventy meters long. A fellow aviator was blown off the end of Siriwo once by that tailwind. His airplane didn't stop until it was upside down off the far end of the airfield. He survived the accident, but the airplane, which belonged to a different agency, was totaled.

Every nerve ending is alive on an approach to a runway like Siriwo, every sense super alerted. As I called "committed to land," my eyes absorbed the windsock beside the runway, the airspeed indicator, descent rate, tachometer, altimeter, and every other gauge all at once. I could hear the wind whistling at just the right pitch over the wings behind the muffled roar of the idling engine. The controls were alive in my left hand and under my feet as the Helio and I danced and swayed with the cross currents and eddies in the wind, my right hand on the throttle now adding, now subtracting power to keep the runway threshold on the nose. I fed in one more small burst of power and felt the ground rise up to meet me as trees rushed by on either side. Then I was down, wheels rumbling, fuselage offering its hollow aluminum thunder in protest as the tail wheel trundled underneath. Soon enough I was stopped and out and unloading the supplies my "customers" had requested.

"Hi, Mrs. Moxness," I said, as she and her kids approached the plane. "Would you all mind standing by for a while? I need to drain fifty-five gallons of fuel into a spare drum so that Mike and I will have enough to get home in a couple of weeks."

"Sure, Paul, take your time."

As I walked to the fuel shed, I saw many bandages on the local people's legs and arms. The Moxnesses had been busy treating the tropical infections so common in this area. I asked her about it once:

"I was overwhelmed with the medical work there," she said, "until one morning when my young daughter told me about a dream she had. She said, "Daddy was out on the front porch of our house. He was putting band aids on Jesus's ouchies.""

"I stopped letting it overwhelm me then," she smiled, "and made room for it in my life."

A story like that makes it worth all the heat and challenges we face! I thought as I walked through the mud to the shed. I turned the key in the lock and opened the door and … no fuel drums. "Who would take two empty fuel drums?" I asked aloud to no one in particular. Nobody in this village would have any use for them.

OK, I thought, *plan B. I'll have to fly over to the Kordesi airfield, an extra forty-five minutes onto my already long day, drop the fuel there, and then go back there to refuel before I pick up Mike in a couple of weeks. Great! Everybody has an extra forty-five minutes in his day to burn. No problem!*

I was about to play a role in God's plan that I could not have imagined in the middle of my frustration when I unlocked that shed. I put the lock back on the door, walked back to the plane and began helping Mrs. Moxness and her kids into the plane.

As we descended into Kordesi, where the Edopi live, the Moxness children did what kids do on any long ride.

"Are we there yet?"

"Mom! I'm hungry!"

I reached into my flight bag, pulled out my lunch, and handed it to Mom, "See if they'd like some of this."

"Thanks, Mr. Paul!" they shouted over the engine noise. I just nodded, but my stomach grumbled! I mused on the Edopi people to take my mind off of it.

The Edopi, like many people groups in this area, are a bookkeeper's nightmare. Their counting system consists of three numbers: zero, one, and many. I and the other pilots that serve the region often end up acting as trustees, counting out what the villager must pay for a flight or a product from town and giving correct change.

One other peculiarity of the Edopi is that they have no specific word for *thank you*. The concept of gratitude isn't missing from their culture. They just lack the nuances of vocabulary that we take for granted. They can't say "thank you" and have it understood by someone who doesn't speak Edopi.

I set the Helio down on the soft, flat, rain-soaked airstrip right next to the river, and eased the plane into the parking and launch area. As I pulled the mixture lever back to stop the engine, I noticed the river was about to overflow the banks. Also, no sooner had the prop stopped spinning than half the village was at the airplane door asking me to take Tuti to the hospital.

This day is getting longer by the minute, I thought. I checked my aggravation with some questions.

"What? What's the problem with Tuti? And why haven't you been using the radio? Why haven't you let me know what's going on?"

"The radio quit last week, and we could not get it to work. We've been praying that a plane would come help Tuti. And now you are here! God has answered us! Come see! Come see him!"

"OK, that's great. We'll go see Tuti. But please get a couple of men to roll those empty fuel drums out of the shed over there and down to the plane. I'm going to need them."

"We will, we will! Just please go see Tuti!"

Mrs. Moxness, like many missionary moms, has some nursing training. She joined me as we trudged down the muddy path and climbed up into the hut where Tuti lay.

Life in equatorial jungles is fecund. All kinds of life, including nasty little microbes that crawl into simple wounds, quickly grow into colonies of infection that can become empires of illness in just a few days. A minor scratch on my hand from the fingernail of a Kiri Kiri man helping me unload the plane - that went untended for a few hours - had me at the doctor the next day, my hand swollen to twice its normal size. As I watched her snip away at dead skin she said, "This is gangrenous. I'm glad you didn't wait another day." That's how I knew that Tuti was in real trouble.

Tuti's knee was covered in a tropical ulcer, swollen to over three times its normal size. A few more days and the infection would go septic, overcoming his body's immune system and killing him.

The smell was very bad. One look and Mrs. M and I agreed, "We can't help him here. Let's get him into the plane and take him to the hospital."

Now I *needed* that extra fuel that I couldn't offload earlier at Siriwo to be able to take Tuti to the hospital. I did not need to drain fuel, just load the patient and fly.

"We're going to take Tuti to the hospital." I said. "Please carry him up to the airplane. You can put those fuel drums back in the shed. I'm not going to need them after all."

His friends put Tuti on a makeshift stretcher and hauled him out to the airstrip. They moved their empty fuel drums back into their shed and locked it while I guided the loading of the sick boy and a man to translate for him at the hospital. We had to get going before we ran out of daylight. I lashed the stretcher down in the cargo area and took off.

We dropped Tuti and his caregiver off in Mulia where there was a mission hospital. As I handed off the stretcher to the attendants, I saw the small scar on my left hand where the doctor had removed the gangrenous flesh and I spoke a quiet prayer, "God thank you that I get to do this. It's so simple most of the time, the medical attention these people need. It's so easy for me and so hard for them. Thank you that I get to be part of this."

One hour before sunset, on a day that began before 5:00 am, I delivered Mrs. Moxness and her kids – who had by then eaten all of my lunch – safely to town. I filled out my logbook and dragged myself home for a big meal and a long sleep.

The very next day the Kordesi airstrip flooded, and the runway became unusable because of silt and logs! Tuti would have died if the spare fuel barrels had been where they were supposed to be in Siriwo.

Three weeks later I was in the office at YAJASI, studying the schedule. *Hey! I'm delivering medical supplies today to the hospital where I left Tuti. If I have time,* I thought, *I'll pop over and see him.*

I dropped off the supplies and jogged down to the hospital. The Doctor said, "Tuti was almost gone when he got here. But he survived. He has been improving all this week."

I made my way to a long room with many beds in it. Tuti was at the far end of the room, still learning to use the wheelchair, when he saw me in the door. He quickly spun the chair around and raced down the room. He grabbed my hand in both of his and squeezed it and looked earnestly into my eyes with a huge smile, beaming out the gratitude for which he had no words.

My own eyes brimmed as I began to understand what my friend was trying to say. "God!" I prayed. "Give Tuti and all of the Edopi people your words in their mother tongue. Give them the ability to know Jesus, to look up to *him* and say THANK YOU for all that he has done for them."

*****

A translation team has been working with the Edopi people for twenty-five years. As of this writing they are nearing completion of the New Testament book of Titus.

I never saw the empty fuel drums again, never knew what became of them. But I do know this: God had used the missing drums to save a little boy's life.

Checklist:

✓ When was the last time your schedule got rearranged, and how did you respond?

✓ See James 4:13-15. How does that instruction change the way you think about your schedule?

The Piper Aztec, our over-water workhorse for many years.
Photo credit: Tim Harold.

13

WHEN TEAM WORK IS LIFE AND DEATH

Maluku Islands, Indonesia

Not again! I thought. *Not now! I have nine women and children on board!* With the shark-infested waters of the south Pacific filling the horizon, the left engine on my Piper Aztec was over-heating, coughing badly, and losing power. I began to nurse the engine with the mixture lever, leaning it out till the temps got too high and then richening it up until it started to stutter. As the minutes ticked by it was getting harder and harder to keep it running.

Not good! I thought. *Not good!*

I'm usually in a running conversation with God in my head, but now I started really praying. Visions of trying to make a successful ditching in open water battled for brain space as I fought to concentrate on keeping the Aztec in the air. "God! You've got to help us!"

Praying wasn't the only thing I did. I got on the radio to my new mechanic. Few relationships are more important to a Mission Aviator than the one he has with his mechanic. Some Mission Pilots do their own work. When possible, however, it's better if one person does the flying and another does the wrenching. The two of them have to be able to work as a team. Lives depend on it.

I had been on the field about ten years and had already lost an engine at sea in this same Piper Aztec. The mechanic who had prepped the airplane back then had missed one crucial procedure. He later had to go home for family reasons. That left me doing the flying and fixing, and I was wearing

---

Position Report - Chicken Foot Syncretism

It is like this, they believe in Jesus … but when bad things happen they slip back into some of their old ways.

I burned my fingers while pumping fuel into the plane, then used a pack of frozen chicken parts to keep my fingers iced. A chicken foot fell out of the bag. Thirty people saw it and caught their breath. Like you would do if you saw me come out of a bar with a lip-sticked lady on my arm. "Ah, ah, ah, Dane I've been doing some evangelism in the bar."

You are not buying it. It's just the same. They caught their breath because they know I am a Christian but could not believe their eyes that I have a chicken foot with me to get rid of evil spirits.

Syncretism, mixing Christianity with any other belief. That is what is going on. When people die for an unexplained reason some revert back to the old ways. That is why it is so important to get the Word in their language. Then they can rely on verses they know instead of something they heard months ago in a second-hand sermon.

Pilot Paul in Papua

pretty thin in the process. The news of another mechanic coming to help was a relief. I felt a great weight lift off my shoulders when Jim Andrew, a very experienced A & P (airframe & power plant technician), arrived in Ambon, though we didn't know each other very well. We were still in the early stages of working together and building a friendship when I had to make the two hour, over-water flight from our base on Ambon, pick up some passengers, and return them to our island.

Someone once asked Billy Graham why his ministry was so successful. He replied, "Find a group of men that you can trust, men who are gifted in their own fields, and grow old together." Good teams are built on trust. Jim and I were just beginning to build that trust but it was going to be tested that day.

Prior to Jim's arrival, the airplane I was flying had undergone repairs (piston ring replacement) to the left engine that I knew would cause it to use more oil for its first few hours of operation. So I had extra oil in the baggage area and made sure the crankcase was topped up before I departed Ambon for the first leg.

Just before the six Indonesian women and three lap children boarded, I checked and added oil to the left engine. Sweat dripped from my chin and soaked my shirt as I strapped the mothers and children in under the blazing equatorial sun. I pointed the nose in the right direction and took off for home three hundred miles away, most of it over the open, shark- infested waters of the south Pacific.

Most airplanes that run on gasoline have a throttle and a mixture control lever. The throttle controls how much air flows into the engine. The mixture controls how much fuel is mixed with that air. Add more fuel, or *richen* the mixture, and the engine runs cooler but uses more fuel. Less fuel, or *leaning* the engine, and it runs hotter but uses less gas. Too rich or too lean and the engine runs poorly, or not at all. Pilots adjust the mixture during flight for best performance and economy.

Scanning the instruments on the way back to Ambon that day, I noticed the oil temperature creeping higher and higher on the left engine. I rested my hand on the blue mixture lever closest to me on the throttle quadrant and eased it forward, watching the temperature gauge closely to see if it would stay in the green, normal-operating range on the dial. It dropped a little. I nudged the lever a little more. The temp dropped again. I was about to take my hand away when a small vibration buzzed its way into my palm. It grew quickly until soon the whole airframe was shuddering as the engine began to cough and sputter and shake in its mounts. *Too rich! The plugs are fouling!* I thought.

My passengers, who had been staring out at the deep blue water below, now fixed their eyes on me. Something was wrong. They could feel it. I mustered a convincing smile, "No problem. Just a little adjustment." They had no real idea of the danger they were in, and I wanted to keep it that way.

I brought the lever back, leaning out the mixture to clear the plugs and stop the shaking, but the temperature shot back up. I pushed it forward, the temp dropped again, but not as far, and the shaking returned.

We were fifty-two minutes from home; I said to myself, *This engine is not going to make it! I gotta do something about this!*

I keyed the mic and called home base, praying that Jim was nearby. Thank God he was. "Jim, I've got a real problem up here."

"I'm with you, go ahead."

I explained what was happening. He asked a few questions. Something in the tone of his voice told me that he *wanted* to tell me to divert to a closer airfield called Banda, but didn't want to make me nervous. Jim was new to Indonesia, but very experienced on Piper Aztecs. Realizing this, I radioed back and as casually as possible said, "You know, I think I'm going to divert to Banda."

"Yeah! Go there!" I could hear the relief in his voice.

We diverted to the nearby island of Banda and eased the ailing Aztec down for a smooth landing. Travelers in Indonesia are accustomed to delays and difficulties, much more so than the average Westerner. The ladies were really hungry by then, so I said, "Why don't you all go into town and find some food and come back in an hour or so and we'll see what's going on and if we can keep going." They smiled, taking it all in stride, and made their way toward the terminal.

As they walked away I dug into the emergency tool kit for a screw driver and began to remove the cowling. Everything was hot to the touch. I reached for the dipstick, but snatched my hand away—fingers on fire! I grabbed a rag and pulled it out of the tube. One look and my knees went weak. A tiny drop of oil hung on the very bottom of the stick. The engine was burning through it so fast that ten more minutes in the air and it would have overheated. We never would have made it to Ambon.

A momentary vision flitted through my head of me on the wing in the water, trying to get six women and three little children out of the swamped cabin and into our little raft with the sharks already circling.

No way! We would never have made it.

As the strength came back to my knees, a lump rose in my throat and tears welled in my eyes. I knew somebody was praying for us! Even wrapped in the rag, the dip stick was too hot to hold for long. I put it back in its tube, looked at the engine almost visibly pulsating with heat, and turned, looking back out to sea.

"Thank you, God."

I delivered the ladies safely home via another flight service and left the plane on Banda. Later, Mechanic Jim Andrew and I flew down to assess the situation and decide what to do. The fouled spark plug on the number four cylinder had already revealed the most likely location of the problem; a compression test confirmed it. We took it off and inspected it and put it back on. We had mistakenly used chrome piston rings in a chromed cylinder, a combination that guaranteed excessive oil consumption. Jim said, "I've seen a lot worse than that. This engine will get us home. If we fill it back up with oil and take it easy and don't drive or push it too hard, it will get us back to the shop."

I looked at him closely for a moment and said, "Are you sure?"

"Yeah, it will get us there. We'll just have to take it easy." The look in his eye and the sound of his voice were all I needed.

"OK, let's go."

With a light fuel load, just enough for the fifty minute flight plus reserves, and just the two of us on board, we took off with full power. Once we were up to one thousand feet I brought the ailing engine back to a loafing rpm, just enough to keep it running. That way, if we needed its power to climb it would be available to us, and keeping it running helped me keep the airplane from yawing toward that side. Just like Jim said, the trip back to Ambon was uneventful.

*****

Jim and I formed a bond that day that has never broken. We had to trust each other out there, and this experience proved that we could. He was saying, "I trust you to get us safely home if something goes wrong."

And I was saying, "I don't want to go in an airplane that's going to come apart. If you say it will make it, I trust your judgment."

Checklist:

✓ What kinds of teams have you worked or played on and what made them good or bad?

✓ How do you build trust with the people around you?

I pulled so hard the throttle knob came off in my hand.

14

DEFINITION OF A GOOD LANDING

Papua, Indonesia

Some mistakes cost more than others. Often the best way to fix a mistake is also the most humbling. That's a tough choice for most men, including missionary bush pilots.

Aviation brings that truth home a little more lethally than most vocations. All pilots know that we take off with a limited set of options for returning to the ground safely. We try to hold on to as many as possible, hoarding them like sharp arrows in a precious quiver, shooting them with careful discretion. Each arrow has a name: altitude, speed, fuel, alternate landing sites, etc. Sometimes our quiver of arrows is reduced to just two. The mountain airstrips of Papua, Indonesia, charge a steep premium to pilots who allow that to happen. They will let you smash up your airplane, which is terribly humbling, or die. But they won't allow you to walk away unscathed.

I had always known that and trained for it and practiced saving my "arrows" for a rainy day. One day I reached back into my quiver, only to find I had no good arrows.

The airfield I was flying into, "Kiwi," is in a boxed canyon, known for treacherous winds. It had already claimed two airplanes in the last few years. One crashed just short of the runway, the other plowed into the rocks at the end of it. Both pilots escaped with their lives, but the point had been made: this place could skewer you in a heartbeat. To

---

Position Report - Working in Wamena

The work and flying were the same, but we based out of Wamena. Ten days of 5,000 feet above sea level made for a cool change of pace in the highlands of Papua.

Our son Mark was not looking forward to the trip. But, after flying around with Dad and hanging out with the local people he asked me, "Dad, can we move to Wamena?"

We stopped at a local market to buy some vegetables. Looking around at the mud and the people sitting on the ground with their potatoes, and the smells, I thought, *this place could send some people from our home country into culture shock.* Then LaVonne stunned me with, "This is a very organized market."

Yesterday, it was a pig on the runway, and today it was rain that kept me from landing. Pray for wisdom in the flight decisions. (134 hours and 187 landings in the last 2 months).

Pilot Paul in Papua

---

make matters worse, the strip was shorter than most. A fully loaded Helio Courier needs at least six hundred feet to land. Kiwi is only about one thousand feet long—not much margin for error. Because I grew up flying in Chicago, the Windy City, I was sure I could handle the winds. Plus I already had twelve landings at the strip in my log book; I felt confident that I could handle it.

Mistake number one: I forgot the most important hour in your log book is the next one. I guess that's why I didn't bother to radio the ground contact. He was already worried about the winds that day and would have waved me off. But I didn't call him—mistake number two.

I cleared the nine thousand foot pass that led to the airfield and began my descent into the valley. The runway is on a little strip of land, about five thousand feet above sea level, that looks like an island rising from the floor of the boxed canyon. There is only one way in and one way out. I looked it over and thought, *OK, no weather, I can see everything I need to see, the wind sock is moving around a little bit, but nothing severe. Let's make the approach.*

I make it a practice to call the checklist out loud to myself as I fly the approach. I had almost completed it, made the turn on final, got the threshold of the runway right on the nose and held it there, as usual, with my right hand on the throttle. Everything was falling into place.

The procedure for landing on runways like this is to maintain the glide path – the imaginary line you are taking from altitude down to the threshold of the runway – by making small throttle inputs. You want the threshold, the place where you want the wheels to touch, to stay in the same place relative to the nose of your airplane. If the threshold starts to drop below the nose it means you're high, you're going to land way up the runway. (That's ok if your runway is really long. This one wasn't.) You reduce throttle a bit until the nose drops and you can see the threshold again. If the threshold starts to rise in your windshield that means you are sinking too fast. You're going to hit somewhere before the threshold in the rocks on the face of the cliff. You add power and this brings you back up on the proper glide path.

Halfway down I called "committed to land." Right then the seat shoved itself hard into my backside. The threshold sank from view. A huge unseen hand, a massive tail wind, was pushing me up, up, up the runway! I pulled back on the throttle. But nothing happened! More of the runway disappeared from view. My hand gripped the throttle like a vise. I pulled harder, harder, and suddenly my hand fell away from the panel. I looked down and the throttle knob had come off in my hand! I just stared at it in shock for a millisecond and then threw it on the floor and grabbed the bare rod sticking out of the instrument panel. Everything seemed to slow down at that moment, like it does when things go wrong in a bad dream. The runway markers kept sinking out of my peripheral vision, the trees tops streamed by at eye level instead of rising past like they were supposed to, and the airplane *kept flying*, staying up in the air when it was supposed to be sinking.

Milliseconds seemed to screech to a halt as I considered my options. I was painfully aware that I had reached that point no pilot wants to reach; my quiver of arrows was down to only two. And neither arrow was the weapon I needed to land with the plane and me both in one piece. I would have to choose. I could follow my instincts and go full throttle to attempt a high-angle-of-attack turn at the end of this boxed canyon, like a crop duster. I could shove that knobless throttle into the panel so hard it would puncture my palm. The wing would stall or clip a tree and send me cart wheeling down the valley to my own death. Or I could force the airplane on to the ground halfway up the airstrip knowing there was not enough length to avoid crunching into the rocks at the end. These are the moments we train for. That's why we call out *committed to land* when we pass the predetermined point of no return. We will eat the humble pie and smash the plane to live and fly another day. So that's what I did – I forced the Helio Courier down, saving my life at the expense of the plane's.

"This is not gonna be pretty!" I said out loud as every muscle tensed for impact.

The wheels slammed into the slick, hard-packed dirt halfway up the runway. Too hard on the brakes and I would slide off into the trees on either side. I let the airplane roll up the pitched slope until the last second and then kicked the right rudder pedal. The tail swung around hard and slapped into the rocks. My helmet thumped the window.

And then it was over.

I pulled the fuel mixture to full lean, shut off the ignition, watched the prop stop and just sat there, until my heart slowed to a normal pace, thanking God for being alive. It took a second or two to figure out why, but I seemed to be sitting at a steeper angle, looking up at the sky more than usual. Further inspection showed that the tail was smashed. The fuselage had broken midway between the tail and the cabin, tilting what remained further back on the gear, pointing my face at the heavens. The repairs would cost about $15,000.00.

They say that the definition of a good landing is any one you can walk away from. This one didn't feel very good at all. I was humbled and embarrassed. But I was alive and undamaged. I promised myself never again to assume I was equal to any windy day, and never, never, to fly into Kiwi without a radio report to confirm conditions.

Two months later, when we were almost through the accident investigation and the plane was being repaired, I got word about a friend and fellow aviator with another organization. He flew into a similar boxed canyon and, like I did, came down to his last two options. With a passenger on board, he tried the crop duster turn. Both men died.

*****

Mistakes are inevitable in this life, and some are more costly than others. But like the proverb says: "Before his downfall a man's heart is proud, but humility comes before honor." Proverbs 18:12.

When it all was said and done and I was back on flight status, my supervisors came to me with a surprising offer. "We think you did the right thing in a crisis. We want you to be an instructor pilot for the new guys coming out. We think you're ready."

Checklist:

✓ When life cuts your options down, which one are you most likely to choose, the humbling one or the risky one?

✓ How are you preparing or training yourself for the inevitable day when you run out of options?

PK-JAA after the hard landing.

PART THREE

PILOT PAUL PRIVATE EYE

Taipei at dusk. Photo credit: Yay photos / Elwynn.

15

THE TAIPEI JOB

Taipei, Taiwan

"The story you are about to see is true, only the names have been changed to protect the innocent." If you've ever seen Retro TV, or if you are as old as I am, you will no doubt remember those opening words from the hit detective series, Dragnet. Dragnet was taken from actual Los Angeles Police Department files. The story that follows here happened to my friends while I was on furlough, thousands of miles away. I have changed the names and a few details in order to protect them. But the rest, I assure you, is true.

Two men, one an Indonesian in his early twenties named Lutut, the other perhaps forty, a Mr. Thompson, a Westerner, shook hands and sat down at a table in a luxurious hotel restaurant in Taipei. The younger man nervously placed a small black satchel under the table as they sat. The other ordered tea, and the two exchanged small talk as they waited for it to arrive.

"It is so nice to finally meet you in person, Mr. Thompson."

"You too, my friend. The internet is a useful tool for finding new markets, but one cannot truly do business without personal contact." The older man smiled but looked past Lutut, at the door, at the other patrons, and out the window. Satisfied that they had attracted no attention he looked back at the younger man.

"Yes. I agree."

"Your father must have great confidence in you to give us the opportunity to explore the potential of this relationship. Does he not travel to the US then? Or speak English?"

The forwardness of this question surprised the younger man, but he didn't give it much thought, "I'm afraid not, but that is why you and I are meeting. As you say, we hope to open

> **Position Report - Ten Stinky Pigs Started a Church**
>
> Seven children in one area died from diphtheria. Some of the people thought it was the work of an evil woman or witch. So they worked her over until she "confessed." Then they slit her throat and cut her to pieces and threw her in the river between the angled rock faces and the big tall water fall.
>
> But men from a neighboring area know the spiritual darkness of this place where the murder happened. They gave ten pigs, at a value of over $1000 each, to sell and buy supplies to build a church in this area.
>
> The pigs stink up the plane. But I tear up and start breathing hard at the thought of loading these dumb stinky pigs because soon the profits will go to bring a beacon of light and freedom from the kind of fear that makes you kill some innocent woman. They will build the church where the locals threw the body in the river.
>
> How about that to keep you wanting to be a Mission Pilot as long as you can breathe.
>
> Pilot Paul in Papua

a new market." Lutut felt proud that his father, Pak Markus, had entrusted him with this opportunity. He wanted to make the best of it.

The tea arrived, and the two men fell silent for a moment. As the waiter departed, Lutut lifted the satchel to the table. "Perhaps you would like to see the gems now?"

"Oh no, dear fellow, not here, much too public. Let us enjoy our tea and get to know one another. Then we can retire to your room for a thorough inspection. Agreed?"

"Yes," Lutut said, reddening with embarrassment at his own inexperience. "Certainly."

About an hour later, the two men emerged from Lutut's room with the satchel, walked casually down the hall, and took the elevator to the lobby.

"A word with your manager please?" Mr. Thompson said to the uniformed clerk.

"May I help you?" The small, professionally dressed man greeted them with a smile.

"Yes," Lutut held out the satchel. "I would like to put this in one of your safe deposit boxes."

"Certainly," said the manager. "Please fill out this form and I will bring the keys. Then you may put your belongings in the box yourself."

Lutut was signing the form as the man returned. Mr. Thompson looked on casually from over his shoulder. "Here are two identical keys for the double-locked boxes," the manager smiled. "You will of course need both to open the box, as they must be left in place to throw the bolt. Understood?" Both men nodded. "And right this way, please."

Thompson and Lutut followed the man into a back room. Thompson handed his key to Lutut, who inserted both into their locks, opened the door, and carefully placed the satchel inside the box. Then he removed the keys and handed one to Thompson.

Returning to the lobby, Thompson spoke first. "Well, I must make contact with my bank and start moving the funds. I'm sure you have things to do as well. Shall we meet back here tomorrow morning, say, ten o'clock?"

Lutut reached out and shook his hand. "Yes! That will do very well. Father will be able to confirm the funds have arrived in his bank by then, and we can both be on our way. It has been a pleasure, Mr. Thompson."

"The pleasure has been all mine, I assure you." The older man smiled, turned, and walked away.

Later that evening, Mr. Thompson sat casually in the hotel restaurant, partially hidden by a potted palm, with a perfect view of the lobby. He sipped tea and watched carefully as the manager emerged from his office, spoke briefly to the night clerk who had just come on duty, and left for the day. He stayed put and continued to watch as Lutut, smartly dressed, walked through the lobby and out into the night. He forced himself to wait five minutes to make sure the young man wouldn't return to fetch something he'd forgotten. Then he stood, grabbed the handle of a single suit case on rollers and, with a hurried air, rushed over to the hotel desk.

"Can you help me, please?"

"I will do my best, sir."

"I've overslept and I am late for my flight to Tokyo and I *must* go now. But I have *lost* one of my keys to the safe deposit box."

"Sir, excuse me, this is very awkward. I must call my manager."

Mr. Thompson's pulse quickened and his hands were starting to sweat, but he kept a calm demeanor. After three attempts to reach the manager, the clerk explained that the key sets were very expensive and that Mr. Thompson would have to pay for the lost key.

"This is the charge sheet for a lost deposit key, sir. As you can see, the amount is $346.00. We have one duplicate, but losing the key means changing out the complete box. I'll have to charge you for it."

"Yes, yes. No matter. Just put it on my bill. I have to go as soon as possible. And please call a cab for me, too."

"Yes sir. Just a moment please."

Five minutes later, satchel in hand, Mr. Thompson stepped into the men's room off the lobby. He breathed deeply to calm himself, peered quickly into the small bag, and dropped it into his case. Then he hurried from the hotel to the waiting cab.

*****

Checklist:

✓   How would you react if you had been robbed in such a way?

✓   What would you say to your son or daughter?

**With Mark and LaVonne ready for some R&R in 2011,
but an earlier furlough turned out to be anything but restful.**

16

PILOT PAUL PRIVATE EYE

Chicago, Illinois

The phone rang at my brother-in-law Ken's house in West Chicago around noon. We were scheduled to be back in Indonesia, but a serious medical condition that LaVonne, his sister and my wife, had been diagnosed with had delayed our departure. After twenty-eight days in the hospital, she was home recovering.

Ken picked up the phone and heard a man clearly speaking Indonesian. The only thing he could make out in English was "Speak Mr. Paul?" Ken handed the phone to LaVonne. She heard a familiar Indonesian voice on the other end. "Ibu (Mrs.) Paul, this is Pak Markus. I need very much to speak to your husband. Is he there?"

LaVonne immediately understood that something was wrong. Pak Markus is a cheerful man, with a spirit of fun in his voice. But the spirit was gone. He spoke with a sobriety she had never heard in the many visits Markus had made to our home over the years. And Markus, the second wealthiest man in our province, was asking for help, another thing he had never done.

> **Position Report - Bad Brakes for Breakfast**
>
> Just before takeoff to one of our most challenging airstrips the left brake "stops" working. Back to the hangar to check it out. A mechanic and I work on it and "bleed the air out of the system." Out again and I am just about ready for takeoff when again the left brake pedal "stops" doing its thing and goes to the floor. As the propeller comes to a stop a second time to fix this brake, a deep breath comes out of me and a "Praise God someone was praying for me."
>
> The Bible Translator has his house right at the end of the airfield. No brakes means the airplane and I could have joined him and the family at the breakfast table.
>
> Pilot Paul in Papua

"Markus, Paul is not here. He won't be back for at least five hours. Is there something I can do?"

"No ... No. We will call him back in five hours. Please ask him to be ready as soon as he returns. Please? We are in great need."

"Yes. I will do that."

Five hours later LaVonne handed me the phone as I walked in the door. "Honey, I think something bad has happened. Pak Markus said he *needs* you."

The phone rang right on schedule. It was not Markus in Hong Kong, but Lutut, his son, calling from Taipei.

"Lutut! LaVonne said your father called. What's going on?"

"Pak Paul, we have been robbed. The man who was supposed to buy the jewels I brought to Taipei has stolen them. If we don't catch him, my family is bankrupt."

"Huh? What man? What happened?"

Lutut launched into a tumbled account of the previous day's business in Taipei. None of the money had been wired to Markus's account, and Lutut could not find Mr. Thompson, the American jewel merchant. The man had simply vanished.

"My father wanted me to explain what happened. He is in Hong Kong. Now that I have told you, he will call you shortly. Will you please wait for his call?" Lutut asked.

"I'll be here, Lutut."

Markus's call came in a few minutes later. I could hear the strain in my friend's voice.

"Paul, the wholesale value of these gems is four hundred and sixty thousand dollars American. When Lutut first called with this news, my wife collapsed, out cold for thirty minutes. I couldn't speak for almost that much time. We are devastated. If we do not retrieve them or get the money we will be bankrupt. When my wife came to, she insisted that I call you. I did not want to do this, but she kept insisting, and after some time I realized that I had no other options. This thief is an American. He knows that I can't speak English, that I haven't traveled there, and that I don't know how the American legal system works. You are the only American that I know I can trust. I *know* that you can find him. Please go to Miami and *find* this man. Catch him when he comes off the plane."

"Whoa, whoa, Markus. I'm in Chicago. Miami is as far away from me as Bali is from you right now. I can't just get up and go there. Besides," I said, "he might come in some other point of entry, most likely California or New York."

"Then go there. Let me wire you some money before my business loans come due and we are on the streets. You can pay the police to go get this guy."

"Hang on, Markus, hang on. That's not how things are done here. *Never, ever* offer American officials money to do their jobs. You'll get both of us in trouble, OK?"

"OK. But Paul, you have to find this man for me! You have to! Please take down the address and phone number of Thompson's business in Miami. Please go there and confront him for me. If I don't get those gems back I cannot repay my operating loans, or my employees, or anything else. We will lose everything!"

"I'll do my best, Markus. I'll do my best." I hung up the phone as something close to nausea washed down my throat and settled into my gut and wondered aloud "How am I ever going to find this guy?"

"Find who?" LaVonne and Ken asked. I briefly relayed the story.

Ken said, "Those gems are gone, man."

"Yeah, I think you're right, but I've got to try something."

"What are you going to do?"

"Go straight to the source. Ken, where can I get a burn phone?"

"A what?"

"You know, a burn phone, a no contract cell phone that can't be traced back to you."

"Oh, that!" Ken thought for a minute and then told me of a new store nearby where I could pick one up.

"Go for it!" He gave me that go-for-broke grin that David must have worn when he marched out against Goliath. "Nothing is impossible with God."

I was back with the phone in thirty minutes and sat down to make one of the strangest calls I've ever made. I said a quick prayer, picked up the phone, and called information in Miami. "Thompson's Jewel Merchants, please."

"What are you doing?" LaVonne asked.

We don't watch much television in Papua, Indonesia, probably because there isn't much to watch. But you can hardly be an American if you haven't seen a detective show now and then. "I'm going to give it my best Magnum P.I."

"Thompson's Jewels. May I help you?" The voice was male with a slight southern accent.

"Mr. Thompson, you have a brother, correct?"

The voice became cautious. I had no way of knowing if he was aware of his brother's actions, but I was assuming the worst.

"I am Smith Thompson. My brother Park is out of the country on business."

"Yes, that's what I'm calling about. Your brother went to meet my friend Markus to close a deal for ten kilos of raw gems. Now your brother and the gems are gone and my friend has not been paid."

"I'm sorry, Mr. Westlund. But I do not know what you are talking about." The man drawled.

"Mr. Thompson, you're his business partner! You must know something! What kind of operation are you running down there?"

"We run a respectable business ..."

"Respectable?" I interrupted. "Mr. Thompson, this is a clear breach of contract. I need you to tell me where your brother is right now so that we can get this straightened out."

Smith Thompson's voice went from cautious to cold. "I am not my brother's keeper, Mr. Westlund. That is all I have to say. Good-bye." The line went dead.

It was just as well. I was growing increasingly uncomfortable with what I was doing. I knew I had no leverage, no authority to lean on Thompson. Another thing worried me as well. I had no idea whether I might be exposing my family or my work to problems that a man with international business connections might cause. Most importantly, I had no inner peace. Strong-arming people is not the way of Jesus.

I hung up the phone and looked at my brother-in-law, Ken. "Do you know any lawyers?"

Ken couldn't think of a lawyer, but I remembered a friend who was an attorney. We spent the rest of the afternoon on the phone talking to our lawyer friend and a retired detective in West Chicago, whom Ken knew from his church. The news was not good.

"He can kiss those gems goodbye, Paul. Unpolished gems changing hands in Taipei between an Indonesian and an American would be a civil matter. The burden of proof will be on your friend. By the time it clears the legal system, Thompson will have taken the best gems. At best Markus will recover fifty percent of the value. And that's before legal fees and other expenses," advised the lawyer. "I'll start some basic legal action and send something on our letterhead to let Thompson know that Markus has friends in the U.S. and he can expect a lawsuit if he doesn't pay. My advice is to tell him to cut his losses and start over."

The detective wasn't much more encouraging. "It will be the proverbial needle in a haystack, Paul. And besides, a smart crook would stash the goods in a locker in Taipei for a while until things died down. If you don't catch up to him before he has a chance to do that, he'll probably accuse the son of having a girlfriend that made off with the gems. No one could prove otherwise."

"OK, thanks," I said. "Is there anything else they can do? Anything else we need to know?"

"There is one thing they have to do right now. They have to get a police report from Taipei establishing ownership of the gems and the fact that the theft happened. Since this is an international crime, the report will go out on Interpol. The Taipei Police are a professional bunch. They'll get it done quickly."

I called Markus as I had after every new revelation and told him to get that report. He made the necessary calls and jumped on a plane from Hong Kong to Taipei.

*****

Checklist:

✓ What is your first reaction when the odds seem stacked against you?

✓ See Joshua 1:9, Acts 27:22, 1 Corinthians 16:13. What do these scriptures teach us about facing overwhelming odds?

LAX, one of the largest ports of entry in the world.
Photo credit: Christopher Halloran.

17

TO CATCH A THIEF

Chicago, Illinois

Things were not looking good for my friend Pak Markus. The lawyers and law enforcement people I had conferred with offered little hope. His jewels were most likely gone for good and his business enterprises would soon follow.

Grasping any shred of hope or help I could find, I decided to call the US Customs Authority in California, Thompson's most likely point of entry. The only number I could find was an 800 number to report drugs. I called and picked the most likely option on the automated menu.

A man answered and listened politely to the jumbled story I had so far.

"You say they are raw gems? Not mounted jewelry? Not drugs? And there's no description of the man or the bag and no proof of who owns the gems? I'm sorry, Mr. Westlund. That's a real long shot. There are 110 international flights a day coming into this port. Most of our time is spent looking for drugs."

Feeling deflated, I hung up the phone and looked at LaVonne, "I don't know what else to do."

"Why don't we pray and get some dinner? You'll think better after some prayer and some food in you."

"Good idea." We bowed our heads. "God, I really want to help my friend, but I don't know what to do. This will destroy him, and he is such a good man. Please give us wisdom. Amen."

Since we were staying at Ken's house we ate a late dinner with Ken and his wife and then I walked out in the backyard to stretch my legs. Indonesians

---

Position Report - Day in the Life of a Mission Pilot

Rain and clouds delayed the departure forty-five minutes. At the first stop, I realized a battery was not properly boxed, leaking acid on the floor of the plane and ruining a hundred pounds of rice.

My next load included a pastor, three church workers, and 275 Bibles headed for Sape. I tried to buy baking soda to help neutralize the acid leak, but there was none available.

Then I flew to a village where missionaries are translating the New Testament into the local language. I traded my lunch for some baking soda and cleaned up the floor of the plane.

The next flight was to take a sick man to a rural medical clinic and drop off a translator in a village twelve miles from his home. His airstrip is not finished, so he would hike the rest of the way.

On the way home, I flew two translation checkers over 11,000-foot mountains. These missionaries completed a Scripture translation and had been checking on the progress of new translation teams.

Checking my fuel, I informed my passengers that we needed to divert to a small village where we have fuel stored; I hand-pumped twenty-eight gallons of fuel into the wings. As I finished my day, I found myself reflecting on what a privilege it is to serve the Lord here.

Pilot Paul in Papua

93

don't wear shoes when inside the house. So I'm used to being barefoot. The thin green fescue felt cool and comforting beneath my feet. I squeezed it up between my toes as I walked around a few tree stumps left over from an earlier storm, studying the best ways to get them up. Ken and I were going to tackle that job in the morning.

As the sun slid slowly through the trees in the west, a thought came to me. *It's 7:30 PM in Chicago. Maybe they've had a shift change at Customs in California. It's an 800 number. What have I got to lose?* I dialed the 800 number again, but this time I chose a different option on the automated menu.

"United States Customs, Pacific Region. May I help you?" The voice was different from the last time I called. *That's positive anyway.*

"Yes, I hope so. I'm calling on behalf of a friend of mine who is an Indonesian business man."

The last time I had called Customs my story had been jumbled, incomplete, and the details were sketchy. This time I had it in order and relayed it meticulously.

"Let me connect you with Special Agent Franklin. She'd be the one to talk to about something like this."

"OK, very good. Thanks."

"Mr. Westlund?" Agent Franklin's voice was firm, confident. I felt immediately that she would be helpful. "I understand you have a story about stolen gems?"

"Yes that's right. I'm calling on behalf of my friend Mr. Markus, an Indonesian business man who has been robbed by an American jewel merchant. We think the man may be on his way through your port of entry."

"OK, Mr. Westlund. Walk me through it from the beginning and let's see what we have to work with."

She listened patiently as I took her through the story.

"I think you might have a case, Mr. Westlund. But I'm going to need more specifics from you and fast."

"OK, you got it. What?"

"First, I need that police report from Taipei. Without it I can't hold him long *if* I can even find him. Have them fax it to me as soon as they get it. Here's the number." The connection broke a little as I wrote her fax number down, but she was talking too fast to interrupt.

"Second, I need a physical description of the man. How tall is he? Hair color, eye color, and the kind of clothes he might be wearing. Is he heavy set or thin? Sharp or slovenly? Is he in a business suit? A polo shirt and jeans? I need to know."

"Got it. Go on."

"Third, what did that satchel look like and how much did it weigh? What did the contents look like? What kind of gems were they? Were they loose? In velvet bags? Mounted in jewelry? I need to know all of that."

"Fourth, what airline was he using? What is his flight number? Where was he going next? What was his itinerary?"

My hopes rose with every word. *This lady knows her stuff!* "OK, will do. I'll call my friend and get back to you as soon as possible."

"Oh, and one more thing, Mr. Westlund: If those gems are in raw form, not mounted in a finished piece of jewelry and he declares them on entry, we have no authority to pull him out of the line. The only way we can detain him is if he has the bag as you describe it in his luggage and fails to declare the gems on the way in or undervalues them when he declares them. Got it?"

"Yes. I got it. Thanks." I hung up the phone discouraged again. *What were the chances that he would still have them all? What if he'd sold them in Taipei or just got nervous and dumped them? Or what if he declares them and walks right through? This is not going to be pretty.*

I called Markus's number again, but he was in the air somewhere between Hong Kong and Taipei. I tried Lutut instead.

"Lutut! Hi! This is Pilot Paul."

"Oh, hello, Paul." The young man was despondent.

"Look, Lutut, I have some news. Tell your dad to fax that police report as soon as he gets it, to Special Agent Franklin with U.S. Customs in Los Angeles. Here's the number. "

Lutut wrote it down.

I held my hand over the receiver and asked my brother-in-law, "Ken, you don't have a fax machine here do you?"

"No. But there's one over at the church. I'm sure we could use that one."

"Lutut, fax that report to me, too, at this number." I gave him the church fax number, covered the phone again and nodded at Ken.

"Lutut says it'll be there shortly." Ken jumped in his car and drove the ten minutes to the church office to retrieve it.

"And Lutut, give me as clear a description of Mr. Thompson as you can as soon as possible, OK?"

Lutut was quiet for a moment, "He is tall and dressed casually, not in a business suit," he explained. "And he is not heavy. He wears black shoes, the slip-on kind, not laced. His eyes are ... his eyes ... I can't remember, but probably green."

Lutut gave me the rest of what he remembered, and I called Special Agent Franklin back, relaying all that I had. With the time difference, she was still at work in California.

"It isn't much to go on, Mr. Westlund, but we'll do our best," she said. "And I still need that police report."

"It's on its way. They have your fax number now."

"Right. I'll call you tomorrow if Mr. Thompson turns up."

I hung up the phone and looked at LaVonne. "Let's go to bed. I'm worn out!" It was midnight in Chicago.

At 1:00 AM my cell phone rang. I grabbed it in a fog, still half asleep and incoherent but wanting very much not to let my concerns interrupt my in-laws' rest. It was Popie, Markus's daughter in Bandung, Indonesia. "Pak Paul, I have some information."

"Mmm, yeah ... OK. Go ahead," I yawned.

"We think Thompson is in Tokyo. We think that he will not arrive in California until four days from now."

"OK, Popie, OK. Thanks. G'night." I dropped back off to sleep, not really sure of what I'd just said.

Ken and I were up early the next morning. After a quick breakfast we were out in his dew-drenched backyard, pick and shovel in hand, ready to dig up those tree stumps. The air was cool and I was eager to work. By 8:00 AM the sun was warming our backs as we dug the shovel into the rich black soil, cut through roots with the pick axe, and looped a chain around the first stump. The day before, with its hours of anxious phone calls, had been frustrating. It felt good to do something with my hands and see the results immediately. I had almost forgotten about Popie's call in the middle of the night.

By 3:00 PM we were in a good lather, with two stumps sitting in the back of Ken's Dodge Dakota pick-up and a third one well on its way out of the ground. LaVonne came outside and called, "Paul! Phone! I think it's the Customs Agent!"

Uh oh! I thought. *I forgot to call her and tell her about Popie's call last night. She's going to be ticked!*

"Hello, Special Agent Franklin! Thanks for calling."

"Hello, Mr. Westlund, I …"

"Hey, I'm really sorry, but I got busy working today and forgot to tell you that …"

"Mr. Westlund, it's …"

"That my friend called last night and …"

"WAIT! WAIT! MR. WESTLUND! STOP!"

"Yeah? What's wrong?"

"Mr. Westlund, we have the gems!"

"You what?" I was so excited that I yelled into the phone.

"We have the gems," she said. It was great news, but she sounded angry.

"We were able to identify him based on the information that you gave us and we have detained him. We have the gem stones. But Mr. Westlund, I am on thin ice. I cannot hold the gems for more than forty-eight hours without evidence that a crime has been committed. I need that police report. You said I would have it yesterday, sir, and it is not on my desk."

"You didn't receive a fax from Taipei?"

"No sir, and I must have it or *I* will be in violation of the law."

"I've got it right here. Give me your fax number again please."

When she read it out I saw the mistake. The fax number I'd given Markus was one digit off.

"We'll send it right away."

"Good. As soon as I receive it I will turn the matter over to the California Justice system. I encourage you to have Mr. Markus's attorney contact the State of California to pursue this matter to a conclusion. Good day."

That was the last I ever heard from Special Agent Franklin. Finally, my friend's livelihood was safe. I looked at my watch, 3:30 PM Chicago time. It would be 4:30 AM in Taipei. I punched in the numbers anyway.

Lutut snatched up the phone on the first ring.

"Lutut, you're awake at this hour?"

"None of us are sleeping well tonight. I had a feeling that you might call, so I stayed awake. Do you have news?"

"Yes, Lutut! We've got the goods! We've got them!"

"You've got them?! You've got them?! Eeeeyess! Pa Pa! Pa Pa! Wake up! Wake up! It is Pilot Paul and he has the gems!"

"Paul? Is it true?" Markus's voice was groggy, unsure.

"Yes, Markus! Yes! US Customs stopped him at the airport and confiscated the gems."

"All of them?"

"Yes, my friend, all of them."

"We *knew* you'd come through. We knew it!"

"No, not me, Markus. I had very little to do with it. This was a needle in a haystack remember? God came through for you. God came through."

"Then I will say amen to that!"

*****

It would take Pak Markus nine more months and forty thousand dollars to work through all of the legal and financial steps to regain possession of his merchandise while maintaining his business enterprises on borrowed funds. Mr. Thompson was charged with grand theft and lying to a customs agent. He pled guilty to a lesser charge and, having no previous record, was given probation and required to reimburse Markus for his losses.

A few months after our return to Indonesia, we were able to visit our friends. Ibu Markus spoke to me then with great conviction. "We are a wealthy family in our country. My children want for nothing. I believe that God allowed us to experience this temporary loss, the feeling that we would now be poor, to teach them not to put their trust in riches, but in God."

I had prayed as long as I had known the Markus family for their relationship with God. So the comment from Ibu Markus was encouraging. But something that would happen four years later gave me even greater hope.

Checklist:

✓ Whom would you call in the middle of the night if you were facing such a crisis?

✓ Having friends requires being a friend. What are you learning about being a good friend?

PART FOUR

WHEN IT'S ALL BEEN SAID AND DONE

Our home on the hill had no water.

18

WHAT TO DO WHEN THE WELL IS DRY

Papua, Indonesia

I'm over fifty years old. Guys like me don't get many opportunities like this. I was talking to God as I reasoned with myself. *I've got to focus on my new job. I've got to become the best Pilatus Porter Pilot I can possibly be or I'm done out here. I don't have any more time to spend on this house! God! You've got to help me!*

The crisis I found myself in was born of two amazing opportunities that had presented themselves in the last twelve months. After eight and a half years of living in the dirty, dust-choked town of Sentani, where the power plant's diesel generators ground out a ceaseless high rpm whine and the sickly sweet stench of refuse fires filled the air, we had been given a gift, really a series of unexpected gifts. We had obtained a small plot of land out of town and up in the hills, where the air was clean and quiet. And through another series of even more unexpected blessings – fifteen thousand dollars' worth of materials donated out of the blue, normally impossible permits granted without fuss, a large financial gift from a donor in the States who had never helped us before – and with all of this we had been able to build a home, *our* home. For the first time in a long, long while, the Westlunds were going to have peace and quiet.

LaVonne and I had spent every minute of our precious little spare time over the last year striving to make our dream a reality. We were both working very hard at the time, in the air and on the ground

> **Position Report - Thank the Mechanics**
>
> LaVonne had thirty-seven people over to the house on Thursday. It was the mechanics and their families. Every time I reach another 1000 hours she has them over to say thank you for keeping me alive.
>
> That day, Thursday, while flying, I got twenty-six thank you's and one job offer. Yes, another mission told me they would buy a PC-6 Pilatus and I could fly it for them. I get thanks and pats on the back all the time but the mechanics just work and take the responsibility.
>
> Back in Feb. I completed a flight and two mechanics were walking up to the plane all greasy and sweaty to ask if everything was alright with the plane, and the passengers cut them off at five feet away and thanked me profusely for the extra effort I made to get them out that day. I was so embarrassed. I said to them, "These mechanics are the real heroes. Thank them."
>
> Point is I get thanked all the time. They get none. So LaVonne had them over for the 11,000 hour party. We thanked them at the potato bar at our place. They are the ones who keep Missionary Pilots in the air.
>
> Pilot Paul in Papua

in support of the mission, and we were near exhaustion with the effort. Every two or three days we would go up the hill and check on the progress of our new home, but we still couldn't move in. Though the home was almost complete, it had no water supply. I had attempted a well, but the technology available to me was too primitive to drill down to the water table far below. Another arrangement, where I would tap into someone else's well and pump it up the hill, had just fallen through. The home was, for all intents, finished. We could see it there on the hill. We could imagine ourselves in it, entertaining friends and fellow missionaries in the kitchen as LaVonne so loves to do. The lease on our current house would soon run out. But we *couldn't* move in without water.

I was out of time to search for solutions. Another unexpected blessing had come to me through YAJASI, the organization I flew for, that was about to demand all of my waking thoughts. After thousands of hours in the air and almost two decades of service in the venerable Helio Courier and Piper Aztec, I was being offered a job I had never dreamed would come my way: flying a turbine powered aircraft.

Mission Aviators aren't wealthy, but we do not take a vow of poverty when we sign on to fly for God. We expect to make sacrifices, but we also expect to provide reasonably for our families. Like every other man pursuing an aeronautical profession, we want to be the best and fly the best. Ten years earlier I had faced a kind of Mission Pilot mid-life crisis. A friend in the States had offered me a turbine job with a large tool-making company's corporate flight department. Shortly thereafter I lost an engine two hours from shore in a YAJASI twin Aztec I was then flying. The offer in the States looked better all the time. In addition, because of the physical demands of mission aviation, most Mission Pilots leave the field by their mid-forties. I had stayed past age fifty. And by staying I felt that I had closed the door on the opportunity to ever fly a turbine.

But now, at age fifty-two, the door was opening. "Ok, Paul," Syd Johnsen, Chief Pilot for YAJASI, was smiling at me as I walked in from a long day in the air, "this is your last week in the Helio. Next week you go full-time in the new PC-6."

From 2004 through 2008, God had answered the prayers of YAJASI in a miraculous way. With our current fleet of gasoline engine-powered Helio Couriers and Piper Aztecs rapidly approaching the end of their service life, and avgas increasingly impossible to get, the aviation ministry had begun to pray for turbine powered airplanes. They were the logical replacement because of their performance, but more importantly, they run on readily-available jet fuel. After a couple of years of fruitless fund-raising, God had provided three of the one-and-a-half million dollar Pilatus PC-6 "Porter" aircraft to the ministry almost literally "out of the blue." Even then, I wasn't sure I'd ever be asked to fly one.

I explained the situation to a visiting pastor friend one night over dinner. "I get this offer, and I'm so incredibly blessed by it. But I'm at what is usually the end of a Mission Aviator's career. I'm thinking to myself: *If I do not excel in this, where am I going from here? I have to put every ounce of my energy into becoming the best Porter pilot that I possibly can be. I have to eat, drink, and sleep this airplane because I'm never going to get another opportunity like this. I don't have time to be trying to solve water problems for my house! God!* I prayed *I'm done! I'm desperate! I don't know what else to do! You've got to help me!*"

A few days later, as grey dawn filtered through our bedroom window, I rolled over and switched off the alarm before it could go off. I lay on my back for a few moments and listened as night faded into day. No generator noise. The power was off again. Then I got dressed, poured myself a glass of orange juice, and sat down in a favorite chair with my Bible. I was reading through Isaiah in my regular devotions, so I tugged the ribbon page marker and opened to the prophet's words in chapter forty-one. My eyes scanned the page until they came to verse seventeen: *"The poor and needy are seeking water, but there is none. And their tongue is parched with thirst; I, the LORD, will answer them myself. As the God of Israel I will not forsake them."* My heart filled up and my eyes welled with tears. The verse resonated with everything in me as I prayed, "That's me, Lord. I'm desperate. I'm leaving this in your hands. I trust you. I've got to go to work now on this transition to the Porter." And that's what I did. I went to work on learning the new airplane and did my best to put the water problem out of my mind.

On my way home that afternoon I stopped at a fruit stand to buy some oranges and noticed a young American man, probably in his mid-twenties, struggling in rough Indonesian to bargain for some mangosteen, a very tasty but expensive fruit. I watched him for a bit and then offered a little help. "You're not going to get mangosteen for that price. It's too expensive for the shop keeper. He's my friend and he can't even sell it to *me* that cheap. These oranges are pretty good though and they aren't as expensive."

One thing led to another, and I said, "Hey, are you walking? Why don't you c'mon home with me and we'll feed you some chili?" We jumped in my car and headed home.

LaVonne was away at the time, so my son Mark put an extra bowl on the table and ladled out the chili as we talked about our work, "Well, I've been wringing your ear off talking about what I do," I said. "What brings you out to Papua?"

"Oh, I'm here with Youth With A Mission, YWAM for short."

"Yeah, I've heard about them. What do you do with YWAM?"

"I work with a project called *Water for Life*."

My ears perked up as a shot of adrenaline coursed through my veins, but I tried not to show it so I casually asked, "What does *Water for Life* mean?"

"Well," he said, "I help villages and individuals and families in areas like this find or develop good clean sources of water. Good water is essential to good health, you know, life. So we call it *Water for Life*."

The little thrill that was running through me just then couldn't contain itself any longer. "Hey, would you mind if I told you about a water problem I have?"

"Sure," he said. Then Mark brought the pot of chili over from the stove and served our bowls.

After offering thanks for the meal, we dug in and the young man asked, "So what's your water problem?"

I described the situation with the almost-finished house.

"How big is the roof on this house?" the YWAM missionary asked.

"Huh? The roof?"

"Yeah, the roof, how big is it? How many square feet?"

"Hmm. Maybe … maybe twelve hundred square feet."

The younger man grinned, "You don't have a water problem."

"I don't?"

"Nope. You have all the water you need. Have you put gutters on the house yet?"

"No. I didn't think I'd need them."

The young man smiled again and asked for a piece of paper to make a sketch, "Ok, here's what you do. You put gutters on the house. Then you build an old fashioned cistern, pipe the rain water into it, pump it back up to a header tank stationed above the house, and voilà! Water problem solved. Now, what else do you want to talk about?"

The next morning I made a couple of calls, set the water project in motion, and then went to work learning how to fly the Pilatus Porter. Three weeks later the water system was in and we were preparing to move into our new home. In the six years since, the tank has never been below half full. We've never come close to running out of water.

*****

That's life on the mission field, just one day to another saying, *God, I'm desperate for you*, and seeing God come through, again and again. That's what I love about being a missionary.

Checklist:

✓ When was the last time you felt desperate?

✓ How hard would it be for you to totally turn something like this water project over to God? See 1 Peter 5:7.

A few of my Kiri Kiri friends.

19

PARTYING WITH THE KIRI KIRI

Papua, Indonesia

On a clear January day in early 2006 a Kiri Kiri boy stopped his play and perked up his ears. Even here, a few hundred feet above the river bed, he could hear the outboard motor, far, far down the valley, churning up the stream. He ran up the trail, across the yet-to-be-completed runway four hundred feet above the vast jungle swamp, toward the head man's hut. "I hear the buzzing on the river!" he proclaimed.

The old man looked at the boy and then across to the unfinished airfield. It would be completed in another month or so. Then his people would get more help from the outside world, faster help, as the airplane would be able to come and go like the birds in the sky. The head man looked forward to that day, even though he did not understand exactly how fast the airplane could go. But he did know, from the sound of the motor canoe struggling against the current on the river, that the village had about an hour to get cleaned up. Then the translator would be there.

"Tell everyone to wash in the river," the head man instructed.

Now, fast forward to a hot day in the middle of 2006. I was setting up the Helio Courier for a landing at Wahuka, in Kiri Kiri land. A Norwegian medical aid worker going into the village to help them with health and hygiene issues sat beside me.

Wahuka is one of the shortest, roughest, scariest airstrips we serve. This landing was one of my last in the Helio Courier before I transitioned to the new Pilatus PC-6 Porter. I didn't want to blow it.

Position Report - Angels on My Shoulders

In 11,000 hours of flying I have never been so scared. On approach to Mambramo a freak wind grabbed the plane and violently mashed it down toward the trees. I did some mashing myself, that is mashing the power lever forward to try to escape. I gave up any idea of landing there and dropped the people off at another airfield.

I was still a bit unnerved when I opened my email that evening. One email from a translator out in Mambramo, said half of his roof was torn off by an extremely strong wind. "The wind picked up my roof just like it was the wing of an airplane and tossed it to the west of my house into a grove of trees." Yes, I know those trees, and yes, I know that wind.

A second email brought tears to my eyes. The subject line read: "Trying to reach you." A friend said, "I had lost your email address, but am praying the Holy Spirit to keep angels on your shoulders every time you fly ... I have the picture of you three on the side of my Computer, and you are right here with me every day. My prayers are sent your way."

Thanks to all of you for praying for those angels to keep us safe and serving out here.

Pilot Paul in Papua

The old Courier pitched down as I cranked in a full forty degrees of flaps and the wings gobbled up more air. With the mixture full rich, I twisted the prop control into the low pitch high RPM position to be ready for a go-around if something did not feel right on final approach. I called out, "Check list complete and gear is down," (even though the gear is welded in place) and descended. The river slid beneath us in the base to final turn. I raised the nose a bit and waited for the self-actuating, leading-edge slats – one of those things that makes the Helio such a versatile STOL (short takeoff and landing) aircraft – to pop out from the front of the wing, curling the airfoil even more and tearing the last ounces of lift out of the fifty-two knots of airspeed that kept me in control. The words *committed to land* came out of my mouth just seconds before a green blur of jungle trees raced by on either side. And then we were down, wheels thundering across the rough ground, decelerating immediately, my feet dancing on the rudder pedals to keep us centered on the runway. Once I was confident we were tracking straight, I added full throttle to climb the steep strip up to the parking area.

But something wasn't right. The Kiri Kiri were running – carrying large gourds and coconut shells of something – running right toward the airplane with great excitement. I was afraid they would run straight into the spinning prop. I quickly pulled the mixture to full lean, stopping the engine before anyone got hurt. They circled the airplane, jumping up and down, yelling and throwing the contents of the gourds and shells at it as they did. *What on earth?*

"What are they doing?" the anxious aid worker yelled into his headset. I heard him loud and clear even though I had just turned the intercom off.

Then, *Splat! Splat!* Mud covered the windscreen. Shells and gourds full of mud splashed over the cowling, the wings, the fuselage, splattering the plane with deep red slurry. *The windscreen? Not the windscreen! I gotta see to shuttle another load in here!* We unbuckled as fast as we could and climbed out to stop them, only to get a full dose of the red muck right in the kisser. The Kiri Kiri were celebrating!

Finally realizing what was happening, I shouted in English to my passenger, "Just go with it! They are celebrating your being here! This is how they throw a party!" *Splat!* Mud covered his face. The people picked us up and carried us on their shoulders all the way back to the village.

It took a while, but I was finally able to convince the people to bring water to help me wash off the windscreen. The men handed gourds of fresh water up to me as I balanced myself on the side of the engine cowl and poured it over the windscreen. As we worked, I explained in English a bit more of what the aid worker was up against in trying to teach hygiene to the Kiri Kiri.

"Before they had an airstrip, the people always knew an hour before anyone from the outside world arrived by boat. They could hear the boat motor that far away working up the river. But about the third time one of our guys landed here, the pilots realized that something awful was going on. The whole place, all the people, stunk enough to gag a maggot. You would pull your shirt up over your nose to try and get some clear air, but it didn't help!"

"What was the smell?" the Norwegian asked.

"Death! The Kiri Kiri don't bury people when they die. At least not right away. Like many people in this region they build a pier, a kind of bier or bed on stilts, and put the body on it. After it decomposes for a while, and especially if it was a man of some power in the village, they go and put their hands in the remains and then rub themselves with it. They think it gives them some of his power or authority."

The Norwegian grimaced as his imagination sketched the scene, "Why did the airplane make a difference?"

"They didn't know how much faster the airplane was than the boat. They couldn't get down to the river to wash it all off before our guys landed." I wiped the rest of the mud from the windscreen and climbed down. "Yuk. My wife's gonna freak out! This was a new pilot shirt!" I shook hands with the aid worker. "I'll be back in an hour with the rest of your team."

*****

After the last shuttle from Dofu to Kiri Kiri and cleaning the windshield one more time, I took off and headed for home base in Sentani. When I landed and taxied up to the hangar, the maintenance technicians looked up from their work and shook their heads. "We just washed that plane! How does he do it? How can he get our sparkling clean airplane so grimy in two hours?"

Checklist:

✓   What kinds of people and places make you feel uncomfortable?

✓   See Luke 5:27-32. How does that story shape the way you think about hanging out with people who make you feel uncomfortable?

When you launch into these mountains, you need to be ready for anything.

20

READY FOR ANYTHING

Papua, Indonesia

P asima is like something from a dream of paradise, one of the most beautiful places that we fly to in all of Papua. The airstrip is located about three thousand eight hundred feet above sea level with the floor of a deep valley dropping two thousand feet below. The valley is comfortably wide for pilots as we circle high above the runway to check that it is clear of pigs and people. It is walled by sheer rock mountains soaring straight up to thirteen thousand feet. Multiple waterfalls rush from various heights along the walls so far above the lush green floor that most of the water is vapor before it reaches the forest. In the deepest part of the rift runs an even deeper, wider river, the color of mocha, strong and urgent on its way to the sea. It is beautiful beyond words. I flew a German photo journalist there once. His English was pretty good, but he ran out of vocabulary for this valley. He took pictures and said, "Wow, wow, wow, wow, wow, wow! Can we open the door to take pictures?"

"No! Sorry!" I said.

"Wow, wow, wow, wow, wow!" For eight minutes straight this guy just clicked and wowed. He was so distracted by the splendor of it all down at Pasima that he forgot about and left his extra lens and case there.

> **Position Report - Arbise**
> **New Testament**
>
> In my hands is the Arbise NT that you prayed would make it here. Praise God. Monday of next week I will fly a plane load of these New Testaments into the village for the dedication on the 5th.
>
> Pray that everything would work out smoothly and safely with all the flights into the short and soft Arbise airstrip. We will need to have twenty-three flights to get everyone there. I will be there for four days just helping wherever I can to get things set up and ready and flying people back and forth to the larger paved airfield twenty minutes away.
>
> Pray for the Scriptures to impact the Arbise people.
>
> Pray for the airplane UCA. We are still fixing the plane that got bent a month ago.
>
> Pilot Paul in Papua

It is magnificent. However, descending into and flying the landing pattern at Pasima reveals a more menacing character. On the downwind leg, paralleling the runway, I fly straight at one of those granite walls, towering above me like a giant anvil, and make the turn to base. On the base leg, my wingtip slides by a gnarled old tree barely twenty feet away, clinging to the side of a mountain. Once past the tree I make the turn on final. There is no margin for error, no room for distraction. I must hit my speeds and altitudes just right or the gaping valley below will swallow me in the mist.

To get to Pasima we usually go first to another town called Wamena, about an hour southwest of our base in Sentani. Wamena, the largest town in the world accessible only by air, is about five thousand feet above sea level. With an eight thousand foot runway, it is a regular stop for many mission aviation outfits. The runway is just long and wide enough that some air freight companies use Boeing 737 jets to haul cargo there. The operators of C-130's and BAe-125's and ATR's and AN-12's that fly into Wamena have all bent sheet metal trying to shoe horn those big planes into this small, high altitude airfield. And the people there have embraced the opportunities presented by aviation. Almost every flight into and out of Wamena is carrying, along with translators and church workers and people going to school or hospital, some kind of produce from the area to be sold in the large markets in Sentani.

With no other transportation infrastructure available, the airplane is a critical link in the area's economic and community development. The arrival of larger, more powerful turbine aircraft like the Pilatus Porter that I've flown since 2006 means even more produce can be moved on a regular schedule, a great economic benefit to the Papuans.

That's what I was doing in March of 2008, a routine run from Wamena, a little over five thousand feet above sea level, down to Pasima. But in the mountains of Papua, nothing is routine.

With a full load of local goods and a few passengers securely on board, I taxied to the end of the long paved runway, ran the final preflight checklist and pushed the Pratt & Whitney PT 6-27 turbine up to full takeoff power. You would never believe that something that sounds so much like a Hoover vacuum on steroids could make five hundred and fifty shaft horse power. But the PT 6 does. Even at this altitude and weight, the Porter fairly jumped off the runway. The wings bit into the blue sky and we were airborne in fewer than five hundred feet.

Thirty feet off the ground, with my left hand on the control stick, my right resting on the throttle lever, I was about to pull the lever back from takeoff power to a climb-cruise setting when BANG! My head slammed forward like it had been hit by a baseball bat. The airplane lurched and my right hand instinctively flew up to feel my head and find what had hit me. "What was that?" I shouted into my microphone. Even with the helmet's protection my head hurt!

As I rubbed my head, I looked up and saw the flap control, about a foot long handle mounted in the center ceiling of the plane, positioned where my head had stopped it, ninety degrees away from where I had locked it in takeoff setting moments before.

The flaps are located on the trailing edges of the wings. They are deployed the way a bird curls the back of its wings during landing and takeoff to give the wing more lift. I had checked and rechecked that handle during the preflight because I knew we'd had trouble with its locking mechanism. Even so, the force of the air pressure on the flaps as we accelerated during takeoff had levered it out of its lock. The airplane pitched sharply, but we had enough speed and altitude at that point not to stall or recontact the ground. Had the lever let go a few seconds earlier things might have been difficult, but the powerful Porter continued to climb. Once at altitude I retracted the flaps the rest of the way to cruise position and called the chief mechanic at our base in Sentani to report the issue. We analyzed the problem together and agreed that I should abandon my flight plan and return to base to have the flap problem taken care of.

That incident resulted in an Air Worthiness Directive (AD), sort of like a mandatory manufacturer's recall in the automotive world, for all Pilatus Porters worldwide. We couldn't fly again, and neither could any other Porter operator, until replacement parts had been manufactured and installed.

I wasn't thinking about the airplane that night as I sat in my living room and reflected on the day. I was thinking about my helmet. My motorcyclist friend and co-author Dane Skelton likes to quote a safety proverb: "All the gear, all the time." It means that wherever you are going on your bike, you wear your helmet and other safety gear every time because you just never know when you're going to need them. Our pilots are trained to do the same thing mentally. Just before takeoff we ask ourselves: *Ready for anything?* That trip to Pasima brought the importance of that mantra home to me in a way I'll never forget. I had been too busy during the rest of the flight to examine it. But sitting there in my favorite chair, running my fingers over it and looking closely I realized that my helmet was cracked from just above my right ear all the way to the top.

I had worn a helmet for twenty-seven years as a Mission Pilot and never needed it until that day. It probably saved my passengers' lives and mine.

*****

Checklist:

✓ How has life taught you to be prepared for anything?

✓ See Ephesians 6:10-20. What is required to be spiritually prepared for anything?

113

The PC-6 panel, not a place where you want to see smoke.
Photo credit: Dane Skelton

21

I THINK WE'RE ON FIRE

Papua, Indonesia

Thirty-five minutes into a fifty-four minute flight, a heavy, oily smell penetrated my nostrils and set alarm bells off in my brain. I looked at the panel—everything was reading normal. I looked toward the floor and a thin but thickening blue haze was rising from under the panel. My heart kicked into passing gear. *We're on fire!*

Every pilot fears fire. Wycliffe pilots are hyper sensitive to it because in 1972 we had our only fatal aircraft accident when one of the first Wycliffe planes to operate in this part of the world went down in flames. The pilot knew they were on fire and was trying to get it on the ground, but he had no way of knowing how *fast* the fire was destroying the structural members of the wing. He made a standard approach in the heavily loaded aircraft in order to land into the wind. But that extra minute of maneuvering was all the fire needed. The right wing folded on the downwind leg. Had he attempted a faster, but more risky downwind landing, he and his passengers *might* have survived.

Lesson: If you think you're on fire, get it on the ground NOW!

Twice before in twenty-five years of bush flying I had smoke in the cockpit. The first was early in my career in 1989. I had launched from a bumpy mountain airstrip in Papua and climbed to two hundred feet when the cockpit filled with an acrid, sooty smoke. Adrenaline surged as I made a teardrop turn, right eighty degrees and then left

---

Position Report - Calling It a Day

Spectacular views out my "office" window today. With scenery like that why would I need a day off?

A couple from a remote village asked if they and their two children could get a ride out to the city. Their oldest child needed some medical help. Yes, of course I would help. They told me that Oto was 5, but he looked no more than 2 years old to me. That was part of the problem. He was just not growing.

It was just a short flight, but 11 minutes away from the city and medical help, Oto went from constant crying to non-responsive. I had my hands full trying to keep the plane upright and coaching mom and dad to keep air going in and out of Oto. (Dad knows some of the trade language but mom knows none.) But, it was no use, by the time we were on the ground, he was gone.

What happened next was just like out of Mathew 2:18. Rachel weeping for her children ... But this was Wamena and Oto's mother weeping for her child and refusing to be comforted.

I could not focus. I had the wind knocked out of me. I called my supervisor pilot and talked it over with him.

Yes, I am a big boy, but my helplessness in the situation was gnawing at me. I told my supervisor I was calling it a day, going to fly to Oto's village and tell them what happened and come home.

Pray for Oto's mom and dad as they deal with this loss.

Pilot Paul in Papua

---

two hundred and sixty degrees, to line back up on the runway I'd just departed. That was when I remembered that I had an old cook stove strapped in the back. The jostling takeoff had shaken the soot loose and floated it through the cabin. I turned back on course feeling a bit sheepish.

The second time was right after GPS was introduced into our cockpits. I was in far western Papua trying to find an old WWII airstrip so that the translator on board could do a language survey there. I was not that familiar with the area. The newly installed GPS was really coming in handy. It was guiding me to the place that God's servant wanted to check out. Then, just like that, smoke smelling of melting plastic poured from under the radio panel. While trying to keep the plane upright with one hand, I quickly looked under the panel, saw the burning wires and ripped them apart. No more smoke or fire. But no more GPS either. I was on my own to find the old outpost.

This third time the smoke was different, like burning oil, not wires. And so was the situation. I had a full load of passengers on board the PC-6. Veteran translators Andrew and Ann Sims had just completed eight New Testament books in the Epo language. The Epo people wanted to have a celebration because this was the first time God's word was in their "speak." And how the times had changed! I was flying four mission leaders in along with a half-dozen leaders from the Epo people to be at this dedication. It used to be that only Western missionaries would fly in for such an event. Now the leaders, as they are in so much of the Bible Translation movement worldwide, are the nationals.

Everyone was looking forward to that celebration; smoke in the cockpit changed those plans.

"We are not going to a dedication," I said as calmly as possible. Everyone in the cabin could smell the smoke. "We are getting this plane on the ground, NOW."

I powered back and switched off everything except the engine, turned toward the nearest airfield and, because the smoke was making it more difficult to see, opened my pilot window. After what seemed like an eternity, but was only about three minutes, we descended to just above the trees. I was ready to put it in the river or *anywhere else* if the smoke persisted, but the smoke was gone so we continued cautiously toward the Terablu airfield.

I knew I needed to call for help, but powering up the avionics in a situation like this is dicey. It means turning on the avionics master switch which feeds power to a number of instruments, anyone of which could be the source of the fire. I put my finger on the power button of one radio and pushed it on for just a few seconds and then back off. No smoke. I pushed it again and waited and then back off. No smoke. Then I turned it on and made a call for help.

"This is Uniform Charley Echo reporting smoke in the cockpit. We are bound for Epo but diverting to Terablu. Does anyone read me?"

"I read you, Paul." It was Phil Nelson, a friend and fellow pilot. "Say again your problem and ETA?"

"Ok, Phil, it is smooooke in the cockkkpit and ahhh 7:52 ETA for Terahahbluuu." My voice was cracking and had jumped up an octave. My heart was pounding in my ears with all the adrenalin of the last few minutes. A few of my passengers were negotiating with God about what they would do if they got out of this alive. One of them wet his pants. Others were having full blown panic attacks. But I didn't have time to worry about them. I had to get us down.

Terablu is down in the swamps, while Eden-like Epo, surrounded by waterfalls, is up at five thousand feet. The pig feast and celebration in paradise would have to go on without us.

Muggy, mosquito-infested Terablu soon came up in the windscreen. Never were any of us more excited about mosquitoes and swamps! We just wanted to be on the ground. Relying on nothing but my back-up airspeed indicator and the seat of my pants, I put the ailing PC-6 down. The wheels made a familiar rumble as they took the full weight of the big plane and all ten of its passengers. Cheers went up in the back. The tension unwound from my shoulders and my gut unclenched when the propeller blades made a last lazy arc in the sun.

It took a while for the folks back at Sentani to learn that everything, including the airplane, was OK. Chief Pilot Syd Johnsen and Chief Maintenance Technician Chris Jutte had radioed the ground station at Terablu, but all that the radio operator could tell them was what he thought he saw.

"The pilot is putting the fire out on the airplane, but everyone is safe!"

I had my head in the engine compartment, looking at every wire, every fuel line, every hose, smelling for burned things. Nothing. Then I moved inside and put my head under the panel. I turned on the master switches for the avionics one at a time and watched and sniffed as my eyes adjusted to the dim interior. Nothing.

OK, time to make that call, I thought. "YAJASI Base, this is Uniform Charlie Echo. Do you read?"

"ROGER!" The reply was almost instantaneous. Those guys were camped out around the radio, really worried about us. "What is your situation? Was there a fire? Is everything OK?"

"We're good here, guys. Everyone is OK. I'm still looking for the source of the smoke, but see no evidence of fire anywhere. I'll call you when I sort it out."

Another pilot diverted his flight and dropped in to help me assess the situation. After taking apart the heating system we found that some oil had seeped into a heater duct. It had a similar effect to putting motor oil in a frying pan and turning up the heat. You get a lot of smoke, but the main danger is you could die of fright; it just scares you to death. We sealed the leak as best we could and buttoned it back up.

I felt a lot better after that and started to load up to go home. My passengers weren't so eager. When we finally made it back to Sentani, they practically jumped out of the plane. I felt like an airline captain, "Please remain seated with your seat belts fastened until the plane stops, the propeller stops moving, and the pilot has turned off the seat belt sign."

*****

Later after our return, I was doing the paper work (SYE Share Your Experience form) that goes with an event like this and Syd came in. He wrapped his arms around me and gave me a hug. Then he did it again! I've known Syd Johnsen for thirty-two years. He is not a huggy kind of guy. But I figured, *OK! If the chief pilot wants to hug you, let him!* And I hugged him back.

And my passengers? Before everyone could leave, we had a prayer of thanksgiving. Even now, months later, one tells me he is still working on getting his nerves back together.

A second passenger was invited to go to another Bible Dedication, but he still loves life on the ground too much to chance it.

"Maybe in another year," he said.

Checklist:

✓ One of a pilot's greatest fears is an in-flight fire. What is one of yours?

✓ Most people don't die in fiery plane crashes. But death often comes unexpectedly. How have you prepared for that day? See Hebrews 9:26-28; John 3:16-21.

Lethal landing combination: low clouds with a bad tailwind.

22

KNOW WHEN TO HOLD 'EM

Papua, Indonesia

Going is easy. It's knowing when not to go, when not to make that extra stop, when not to attempt that landing, when not to even leave the ground—that's the hard part.

It's hard because the translators and Papuans need us so badly and we want to help so much. And it's hard because Christians live on hope. But pilots, even Christian pilots, cannot afford to do that. We have to be able to look into the future, to see the invisible dangers before they rise up to smite us, and decide, like the old Kenny Rogers song says, *"when to hold 'em and when to fold 'em."*

Seeing into to the future, anticipating what could happen, and making those decisions is the biggest challenge of bush flying, like that day in May 2011, when a translator, his family, and two literacy workers really, really wanted to leave Moyeba.

Moyeba is a mountain airfield where we can only fly at certain times of the day, when the wind is relatively calm. After about 10:30 AM the field gets too windy to land. At some places like Nipsan you can set your watch to an up-valley wind whistling in like a locomotive at 9:00 AM. So we established a wind curfew in Nipsan. After a certain time of day, we do not attempt to land there. Nonetheless, there are times of the year when the wind stays calm all day, so we just check the wind to see how it is doing before landing. The normal pattern is down-valley winds during the night and up valley winds during the day. Most of the mountain fields are built so you land going uphill and take off going down, and that

---

Position Report - Mission Cook had a dream

A lady I know cooks for a helicopter mission organization. She makes the noon meal for 25 to 35 people. Occasionally, I buy lunch from her. One day she asked, "Do you have any more of the great oatmeal date cookies that LaVonne makes?"

"You're from the other religion. You know we can only buy dates during the fasting month."

She replied, "I was from the other religion, but seven years ago I trusted Christ."

"How did that happen?"

"I was in the hospital for more than a month and could not get up or walk. I had a recurring dream. In this dream, I was told to hang on to the Cross, hang on to Jesus and I would walk. I asked a Christian friend what the meaning of the dream could be."

The friend said, "Follow that dream and pray and trust Jesus to heal you."

"I did and I have walked with Jesus ever since."

Also, to put it in mild words, her family does not like her anymore.

I want you to meet the Lady that is hanging onto the Cross and her Lord.

Pilot Paul in Papua

means the wind is on the tail when landing. The prevailing winds are great for takeoff, but in the wrong direction for a landing.

I did my best to get there in time, but a stiff headwind held me up. After two fuel stops, dropping people off at another station, and three hours and forty-six minutes of flight time, I knew I was just too late to land safely. I could see the family with their neatly stacked suitcases and boxes ready to load, gathered at the edge of the field. I could see the MTTs (Mother Tongue Translators) standing with them, ready to go to a translation workshop in town that would start without them if I couldn't get there in time. I could see all of their plans put on hold for a day if we did not make it. I could imagine their sad faces. They had a schedule to meet; I had to try. The turbulent air tossing the plane around on the flyby clued me in to the fact that the wind was already up.

The tailwind maximum for that small airfield with the dogleg right at the beginning is five knots. I made four attempts. The first approach showed nine knots of gusty tailwind, the second showed twelve, eighteen on the third, and nineteen on the last. On that fourth and final go around I had attracted quite a crowd eager for the plane to land. But I had to give it away for another day. I just couldn't land safely with that much tailwind. I hated doing that, leaving them on the ground. Watching me fly over them like that and then fly away was like hearing the bell of the ice cream truck only as it is leaving your neighborhood. I had no choice.

I flew to a larger town thirty-eight minutes away and spent the night. Even launching from there the next morning would not make the decision-making process any easier. If I left too early it would be foggy and I wouldn't be able to see the airfield. If I left too late the winds would be at it again.

"You're staying in our village tonight, Mr. Pilot?"

"Yes, it looks that way. I'll sleep in the plane."

"No! No! Mr. Pilot! You will stay in our house tonight. We'll make you some dinner (sweet potatoes). We'll pack you lunch for tomorrow."

I woke up early, splashed some water in my face, and went outside to check conditions. *Fog*. Nothing to do but let it burn off. As the last shreds melted in the rising sun, I was buckled in, flipping switches and initiating the startup procedure. The "vacuum cleaner on steroids" whine of the Pratt & Whitney PT6A turbine hanging way out on the Aardvark nose of the PC-6 always attracts a crowd, and today was no different. I released the brakes, gave a wave to the crowd, and launched knowing that much of Moyeba would still be shrouded in cloud.

Finally, I was on approach again to the little doglegged field. The far end was still in the cloud, but at four hundred feet above the ground I could see the threshold. My passengers were already eagerly waiting, like they could hear the ice cream truck coming right down their street. I touched down as lightly as possible, because landing on wet grass is like landing on wet glass. The nose began to creep off to the left, but I dared not touch the brakes. I was already holding full right rudder to counter the drift, but it wasn't enough. A little power, a little blast of air flowing over the rudder, now she was back on center and slowing to a walk. I breathed a prayer of thanksgiving. I was twenty-one hours off schedule, but my passengers were just as glad to see me.

Some of the people of Moyeba really needed a ride to the town I'd just left. Sixty minutes later, and after unloading my first passengers, I was back on approach to Moyeba.

The grass would be dry, but now the winds had picked up. I did a low pass and watched the GPS. Six knots, five knots, six knots, the GPS gives me the ground speed numbers to figure against my airspeed indicator's readings and calculate the tailwind. I can't land at six. Five knots! There it is! I stopped looking at the GPS and put it on the ground.

By the time everything was loaded and all the people were on board, the wind had begun to howl, but it didn't matter. Now it was on the nose, not the tail, a headwind. Between that and the five-hundred-fifty-horsepower Pratt & Whitney engine up front, we took off with no control problems and climbed like an express elevator.

Now the winds that hampered us were helping us. Instead of the normal ground speed of 133 knots (154 MPH), the GPS was reading 176 knots (201 MPH), a forty-three knot tailwind! I did the math and turned to look at my passengers.

"At this speed we can make it to Sentani in two hours and twenty-one minutes. Is that OK for the next potty break?"

Everyone smiled and nodded. Thumbs up! Keep going!

For the next two hours I carefully tracked fuel burn and ground speed. The winds never let up, and we arrived in Sentani in record time.

*****

Sometimes, when I tell stories like this, people ask me why I go to the trouble of staying out in remote villages overnight, dodging dicey weather and landing on mountains with a tailwind. You have to know the Papuan people. They feel forgotten by the world and by God. Our work lets them know that they are not forgotten and speeds his Word to the unreached peoples of Papua.

Checklist:

✓ How do you "know when to hold 'em, know when to fold 'em?"

✓ See Matthew 19:28-30. What kinds of things are important enough for you to miss a night at home?

Jakarta, it isn't bad. It just isn't Bali. Photo credit: Yay photos / warrengoldswain

23

MISSING PARADISE, FINDING GOD

Jakarta, Indonesia

Four years had passed since the jewel heist. We were returning from a later furlough to the States. The Markus family had hosted us for three days at a beautiful resort in Bali on our way out of Indonesia. For some reason, when booking flights back into Indonesia, I'd routed us through the capital city of Jakarta instead of Bali. Bali is a resort island paradise that caters to travelers. Jakarta, seven hundred and fifty miles west of beautiful Bali, is a busy, stressful, and crowded place. It's not that it is ugly. It just isn't Bali.

My wife LaVonne loves me dearly and will follow me anywhere, but she chided me a bit for that oversight. "What were you thinking? We have to lay over for a couple of days anyway. Why Jakarta?"

"I don't know. I guess I just wasn't thinking."

It was October 12, 2002. I went out early the next day to jog a bit and picked up a newspaper on the way in. The headline read: BALI BOMBED! 202 DEAD.

LaVonne took one look at it and said, "I'm so glad you weren't thinking!"

*****

As was his custom any time we were nearby, Markus made the five hundred mile flight from his new home in Surabaya to visit with us in Jakarta. While my son Mark and LaVonne shopped, Markus and I had lunch together.

Position Report - I feel your prayers

Yesterday: late start to a long day, bad weather, then worse weather. Two hours out I stopped for fuel and twenty extra gallons in gas cans to put in the tanks when we landed at the next postage-stamp-sized runway.

Just before landing the rain stopped and so did the radio. I landed and set my stop watch. Home base will start a search for me in fifteen minutes if I do not call in on the radio. We got the missionary on the plane in twelve minutes and took off into the same bad weather we came through.

As the clouds closed in around us, two passengers grabbed onto the arm and shoulder of the missionary. I wonder if they were thinking, *this missionary is always talking about God. If we crash we will surely go to heaven because we are hanging on to this man.* (A commercial plane crashed here last week killing the Aussie and Croatian pilots, so everyone is scared.)

For an hour and a half, these passengers hung on to our fellow worker as we bumped along in the clouds to our next stop. 958 miles and 8.5 hours of sitting in the plane to get a translator out from his village. Yes, I feel your prayers with me.

Pilot Paul in Papua

We were just finishing the meal and talking about the bombing when my friend changed the topic. "Something in the Bible has troubled me for a long time," he said.

"What's that, Markus?"

"It is one of the sayings of Jesus, Matthew 19:23 and 24," he said. "I tell you the truth, it is hard for a rich man to enter the kingdom of heaven. Again I tell you, it is easier for a camel to go through the eye of a needle than for a rich man to enter the kingdom of God."

The verse resonated with me and triggered a memory of a discussion about it at Moody Bible Institute all those years ago in college. "What troubles you about it, Markus?"

"I am a rich man, Paul. I think that I love God. I try to serve him. But these words of Jesus trouble me. Will I enter?"

Markus was telling the truth. He was a very wealthy man by Indonesian standards. The look on his face told me this was not a casual question for him either. Hearing it sent a thrill through me because it was the question I had waited and prayed about for my friend for seven years. I longed for Markus to know Jesus the way I knew him, to have the hope and peace and joy that I knew in my relationship with God. That is not the kind of discussion that can be forced. Now, Markus had opened the door.

I whispered a quick prayer then spent a few minutes walking him through what I had learned in college about the verse. Then I pointed him to the ones that follow.

²⁵"When the disciples heard this, they were greatly astonished and asked, 'Who then can be saved?' ²⁶Jesus looked at them and said, 'With man this is impossible, but with God all things are possible.'"

"Markus, were it left up to us, none of us would qualify to enter the kingdom of heaven. Fortunately it isn't up to us. Jesus died for our sins so that if we believe, repenting of our sins, we will be saved. With man it was impossible, but God has made it possible for those who will believe."

I prayed as I spoke that my friend would comprehend.

He listened quietly and then looked away thoughtfully for a moment. "I believe that," he said.

"I am so glad you do, my friend. I am so glad that you do."

*****

Checklist:

✓ If you died tonight and had to face God would you be allowed to enter? Why? Jesus said, "I am the way, the truth, and the life. No one comes to the Father except through me." (John 14:6).

✓ If you were to face God tonight and he were to ask this question, "Why should I let you in to my heaven?" how would you answer him?

A Papuan Bible dedication celebration.

24

WHEN IT'S ALL BEEN SAID AND DONE

Papua, Indonesia

"Owwooo! Ouch!" I involuntarily yelled. Hundreds of heads turned in shock and concern at first. Then they burst out laughing. It was so embarrassing! Camera men are supposed to film the action, not be the entertainment. Yet here I was the rock-star pilot who had just the day before helped deliver two thousand copies of the Bauzi New Testament for this dedication celebration, and instead of silently filming the solemn ceremony, I'd become the center of attention. I couldn't help it either. My backside suddenly felt like a dozen bees were in my britches! I'd backed into a sago palm while trying to get a better shot of the podium. Now a bunch of the needles were stuck in my rump!

Bible dedications are my favorite part of life on the field. It's the fulfillment of all of our dreams and hopes, the day we deliver God's Word in the mother tongue of a people who've never heard him speak their language before. It signals the completion of so many dreams and seeds, the hopes of so many people, not only us, the translators and support workers and aviators, but especially for the Papuan people themselves.

Many of the Bauzi people, especially the ones who had helped with the translation, already understood the liberating power of the message of Jesus. They had been freed from constant fear and oppression from evil spirits, and spirits of dead relatives. Nearly everything they did was colored in some way by this terror. God's Word set them free from it.

In the message of Jesus they found freedom from constant infighting and never-ending revenge and "pay-back" killings between clans inside the language group, and on language group borders, between people groups.

In God's Word of reconciliation they found freedom from fear of and hatred towards one another such that much more cooperation and collaboration became possible between villages, and even whole territories. This released energy and time for them to invest in pursuit of a host of other positive things and opportunities like cooperative farming and fish farms. Trade and social interactions between villages and wider areas throughout the region vastly increased. Travel throughout the language area increased, by ground and by air, due not only to the airplanes, but also because they no longer feared being attacked by their neighbors. Openness to complete outsiders (coastal communities, government officials, and people coming into the area from other regions of Papau) increased, which also increased opportunities in economic, social, and educational development.

In God's Word they found a better way to live as families and communities. For the first time men, women, and children could live in a single dwelling all the time if they wanted to, which their fear of the spirit world had never before allowed. Respect for and treatment of women, especially allowing them complete access to the spiritual life of the community, increased dramatically. Suicide rates among women, who as a class lived in utter despair most of the time, greatly diminished. Child abandonment and infanticide generated by centuries of fear of the spirit world virtually disappeared.

It isn't in the news as much as it used to be, but there was a time when social anthropologists and other academics vigorously opposed Bible translation and other kinds of mission work among people groups like the Papuans. My friend Dane Skelton experienced this first hand when he visited us in Papua. Dane is a pastor as well as a former automobile technician, so he wanted to bring a gift that would help us maintain our new Pilatus Porter PC-6 airplanes. He decided on a digital camera that could be coupled to a bore scope used for scanning the innards of the Pratt & Whitney PT-6 turbines. He sent out a request to his email list asking for donations to pay for the $1300 camera. Plenty of people helped, but one friend offered an unexpected reply:

"We're really impressed that you believe in what you're doing, but we aren't going to send any money to help. The reason is that we think the Papuan people's religion is as good as anything in the West. It stands to reason that with our advanced technology and medicines that they would want to adopt your religion, but we don't think that Christianity is any better than what they have. We think you should leave them alone."

That response intrigued Dane. He decided to find out what the Papuans thought about it. On a visit to the Ketenban region he asked his translator to pose the question to a Ketenban man. "Some people say that your religion is as good as Christianity, that we should have left you alone. What do you say to that?"

The translator and the Ketenban man talked for a few minutes with increasing astonishment registering on the Ketenban man's face and in his voice as he comprehended the question. Finally he turned and looked at Dane and said through the translator, "How could anyone ask such a foolish question? Don't they know we used to *eat* each other?"

A Bauzi man named Tomat, whom I met the day before the dedication ceremony, is another good example of how the Papuans feel about Bible translation. He had been a champion of the work almost from the start. When my friends Dave and Joyce Briley, the translators who brought the Bauzi New Testament to completion, were looking for help, Tomat had pitched in early and stuck with them all the way through to the end, no small feat for a man who lived on hunting and subsistence farming. He had also endured spiritual opposition and the skepticism of his people. Now his dreams too were being fulfilled. We had no idea how powerfully he felt about it until that day before the dedication. Our airplanes had delivered the boxes of completed Bibles, but Dave wanted to hold the distribution until the day of the dedication. It would give the celebration a bigger impact to hand out all of those Bibles at once. Dave and Joyce had also worked for years for this moment, not only in translation, but also in literacy training so that the Bauzi could actually read their new Bibles.

Tomat didn't want to wait. "Please Dave, please, I want to see God's book with the skin on it. Please. You must not leave it in the boxes. I just want to see it. Just once, then we can put it back."

Tomat is a dear man. He is also persistent. Finally, Dave gave in. What happened next caught us all by surprise. Tomat's eyes filled with tears and his voice sobbed out soft praises, "Oh God who made all things, who sent our friends to give us your words, I give you thanks this day for all that you have done, for all of the people who have worked so hard for so long to bring us your words. How I praise you!"

Now it was dedication day and the ceremony was in progress. Tomat, along with hundreds of his tribe, had his Bible to keep. Songs were being sung. Prayers were being offered. But I had thorns in my britches.

"Help?" I squeaked. Then they all broke up laughing again. "Can someone please pull these things out?"

By the time they finished, we were all laughing our heads off. Not just because of the ridiculousness of my situation, but for the joy of the day. We celebrated like true Papuans that day. We painted our faces and danced and sang in the great circle of stomping feet that mark all such celebrations. We feasted, told stories, and remembered with each other all that God had done to bring his word to the Bauzi.

Finally, it was time to go, time to fly back to Sentani. I did what I always do when a new translation is finished. I took my copy of the Bauzi New Testament and had Dave help me find my favorite verse, 1 Peter 5:7, the word that had sustained me all these years as a pilot in Papua: "Cast all your cares upon him, for he cares for you." I took the Bible around to all of my Bauzi friends and had them read that verse to me in their own language. Then I gave them my pen and had each one write his name or make his mark on the first page. Those Bibles, the Bauzi, the Ketenban, and all of the others filled with the names of my Papuan friends are my favorite things on Earth. I packed it away, loaded the plane, and took off for home.

*****

The End

Paul Westlund.

Final Position Report:

Paul Timothy Westlund, 57, was welcomed into heaven on Sept. 22, 2011, as a result of an airplane crash while serving as a Missionary Pilot in Southeast Asia. Paul was born on June 14, 1954, in Minneapolis, MN, the son of Howard and Lois (nee Foss) Westlund. He married LaVonne E. Martin in 1979. Paul attended West Chicago High School and later graduated from Moody Aviation with a BS in aviation in 1981. He became a member of JAARS Aviation and Wycliffe Bible Translators in 1983, and began serving overseas in 1987. Paul was an exceptional husband and father. He loved to surf, exercise, and build and fly model airplanes. Paul was an animated storyteller and would become emotional nearly every time he got to the crux of his storyline. Paul faced many difficult trials during his overseas service, and yet he could regularly be heard saying, "Isn't this just the best life a guy could have!" Paul is in heaven now because he gave his heart to Jesus.

EPILOGUE

The first time I met him, standing on the top of a mist shrouded runway in Okbap, Papua, Pilot Paul asked me an intriguing question: "What does every red-blooded American boy of fifteen want more than anything else? What is he looking for on his sixteenth birthday?"

"That's easy," I said. "He wants his driver's license and a car. I got mine on the day I turned sixteen."

"That's how much the Papuan mountain folk look forward to having their airfield," he smiled. "It opens up the whole world to them."

A man who knew and worked with Paul for many years, Bible Translator Andrew Sims, explains the significance of that statement and the impact of Paul's life on the Papuan people. DS

A Bible Translator explains Paul's impact on the Papuan people

One of the paradoxes of life in isolated areas of Papua is that "insiders," people from these areas, probably value and appreciate aviation at very near the top of any conceivable list of advantages they now enjoy and benefit from and which are absolutely critical to many aspects of their current life and development.

"Outsiders"—people not living in these isolated areas—perhaps undervalue the impact of aviation in general and of pilots in particular in terms of their personal impact on a host of people they interact with. Pilots like Paul with a huge capacity to love and appreciate people for who they are and as they are, just maximized that impact to the "nth" degree. He was always willing to go the extra mile to help them, and they always loved him for it.

Aside from people like translators, literacy and educational workers, development and/ or health workers who come from the "outside'" and actually live longer term in these remote communities, pilots are certainly at the top of the list among the others who are most frequently contacting, interacting with, and influencing isolated peoples for good. Paul was absolutely superb at doing that. He was as well loved and enjoyed by the people he served as perhaps any pilot here ever has been.

Paul loved Bible dedication ceremonies and loved to have a part in delivering God's Word for them. He used to very frequently carry a copy of the Ketengban New Testament with him in the plane and ask dozens, probably hundreds of people among them to read from it, or to sign it, or to just talk to him about what they loved about it and what a difference it made to them. He would do this with passengers on his flights and with the dozens of people who always gather at airstrips to watch planes come and go. Among many other things, this helped people to see and experience how highly he valued God's Word and how much he wanted them to have it, to be able to understand it and benefit from it.

Despite loving dedications and celebrations surrounding the delivery of scriptures, Paul, several times that I know of, gave up a chance to attend a New Testament dedication himself, in favor of allowing someone else to attend, or to go somewhere else that required a plane or his services as a pilot. He was so unselfish in that regard. But when he was there, and he was for several celebrations we were a part of, after taking care of his passengers and the safety of the plane, he would be bounding all around the area with a huge grin on his face, and taking pictures, laughing and joking with people, dancing and hooting with them, eating the foods offered (no matter how weird or unhygienic), allowing himself to be painted, embraced, or whatever—just totally entering into the experience with the people with his whole heart and person.

It will always be a sadness and deep disappointment to me that he was not able to live to see the dedication of the Lik New Testament and the finish of the fifty percent of Old Testament for Ketengban and to attend those dedications, since he and LaVonne had done so many things to help and support us as translators and to assist so many of our Ketengban and Lik friends for so many years. Upon his death, hundreds who lived in Sentani came to mourn him, and those who lived in the mountain villages held special days of prayer and had feasts to thank God for Paul. All of this memorial activity was very widespread throughout both the Ketengban and Lik areas.

Andrew Sims |
Translation Consultant & Project Facilitator
God's Word Transforming Lives In Every Language—In This Generation
The Seed Company
3030 Matlock Road, Arlington TX 76015
Tel: 704-843-4994
www.theseedcompany.org

Benediction

THE MYSTERIES BELONG TO GOD

Spiritual reflections on Paul's final flight

A s Paul's co-author I'd like to thank you for reading Papua Pilot. His family and I hope that it has inspired you to become a supporter of the Bible Translation movement, and served to move you closer to God.

It has been one of the greatest privileges of my life to put Paul Westlund's stories in print. However, if you've read this far there is very likely a question gnawing at the back of your mind, the same one that overwhelmed all of his family and friends when we heard of his death: How could this happen? How could such a marvelous man of God, an aviator with so much experience and skill, a man totally committed to safety in the air, with 11,000 hours of flight time, crash and die? Did the God of 1 Peter 5:7 "Cast all your cares upon him, for he cares for you," which was Paul's life verse, suddenly stop caring for his servant?

We think not.

A safety report on the crash that took his life has been issued by SIL / JAARS Aviation, the mission that Paul served under. The men responsible for that report are high time jungle pilots themselves, experts in their field, and knew Paul very well. They have a responsibility to get all of the technical data and analysis correct, not only for the family's sake, but for all of the other aviators who can learn from Paul's experience. The pilots reading this will want to contact the JAARS Safety Officer for a copy of the report.

I am a student pilot and thus not competent to comment on the technical issues. However, I have been a pastor for almost as long as Paul was a pilot, and I've had many encounters with unexplainable, accidental death. In each case the issue of life or death usually comes down to a unique set of circumstances, often micro-second timing. A would-be victim steps to the right a fraction of a second before the falling hammer that would surely have killed him had it hit his head, merely cracks his clavicle. A driver rounds a curve at just the right moment and, seeking to avoid a collision in one lane swerves, plowing into a bicyclist in just the right place at just the wrong time, killing him instantly. A pitot system obstruction that could have caused a fatal airspeed error on approach to a dangerous runway mere minutes before becomes a nuisance on approach to a long runway. A few seconds, a few moments, one way or the other, and someone lives or someone dies.

From our point of view these events are completely random, but not from God's. With that in mind allow me to share with you some conclusions that his wife LaVonne, his brother-in-law Ken (who is also a professional pilot), and I have drawn. We hope they will give you the same comfort in facing unexpected loss that we have found.

First, Paul was not being irresponsible or reckless as a pilot. If you've read Papua Pilot you have a sense of how he approached his work. He was a professional aviator. When it came to flying he "kept his powder dry," his options open. It is easy, and no doubt tempting for hangar pilots, to say that he made a mistake. Perhaps he did. Perhaps he didn't. We weren't in the cockpit that day. No one but God knows exactly what events transpired to drop that airplane out of the sky, or the choices Paul came down to in those final moments. And no one but God knows whether we, in the same circumstances, would have made the same decisions.

Second, those of us who have committed our lives to the service of the Kingdom of God know from the Scriptures that we serve at the King's pleasure. In the early days of the Church, the Apostle Peter was miraculously delivered from jail, and almost certain execution, twice. But, in the providence of God, the Apostle James was executed. The Apostle Paul miraculously survived shipwreck and snakebite, but eventually lost his head to a Roman executioner. The same God who protected Peter for his purposes allowed James to be removed from the scene early, or at least, it felt "out of time" to the members of the early church. The same God who protected the Apostle Paul from the ocean and the snake allowed him to die at the hands of the tyrant. We serve at the pleasure of the King of Kings and when he decides it is time for us to go Home, we go Home.

Third, Matthew 10:29-31 speaks specifically to me, regarding the life and death of my friend, because it is the passage that came to me so clearly on the first day we met. Paul had just flown my group into the village of Okbap. He had finished his work for the day and was preparing to spend the night with us in the mission cabin. That's when he told me the story that ignited my writing ministry, the story that became chapter ten in this book, "Wounded Sparrow." Jesus said, *"Are not two sparrows sold for a penny? Yet not one of them will fall to the ground outside your Father's care. And even the very hairs of your head are all numbered. So don't be afraid; you are worth more than many sparrows."* (emphasis mine).

The lengths to which God went to demonstrate that care for my friend and his family were extraordinary, even on the day of his death. The following facts attest to this: There are very few roads in Papua, Indonesia. When airplanes crash there they are usually very difficult to find, much less do any kind of rescue and recovery of the victims. Finally, there are almost never any witnesses to help sort out what happened. The crash that took Paul's life happened within fifty meters of a remote mountain road. There were witnesses nearby. One of the witnesses was a man who knew Paul and who was able to get to the site just moments after the crash. This man began praying for Paul right away and recording interviews with other witnesses. He also had a satellite phone on which he immediately called for help. Proximity to the road meant that Paul's body was not left long in the destructive jungle climate. A smoldering fire that had begun in the engine compartment was extinguished by the witnesses before it could spread. The airplane was sitting upright, almost completely intact, which aided the accident investigation. In short, many unusual things came together in the moment to minister to Paul and give comfort to his family during this traumatic event.

What are we to make of all of this? Just what the prophet Isaiah wrote in the passage LaVonne read in her daily devotions, mere moments before she learned that Paul had crashed.

" 'My thoughts are nothing like your thoughts,' says the LORD. 'And my ways are far beyond anything you could imagine. For just as the heavens are higher than the earth, so my ways are higher than your ways and my thoughts higher than your thoughts.'" Isaiah 55:8-9, New Living Translation.

The mysteries belong to God. He knows the day of our arrival on this earth, and the day of our departure. The timing may seem strange to us, but our thoughts are not his thoughts. The fact that God impressed these verses on LaVonne's heart mere minutes before her life partner left this earth is a source of great comfort for all of Paul's friends and family. We hope it will be so to you as well.

Dane Skelton
February 10, 2013
South Boston, Virginia
daneskelton@hotmail.com

CPSIA information can be obtained
at www.ICGtesting.com
Printed in the USA
LVHW111231010621
689031LV00004B/184